*Praise for Too Damn Dumb to Think . . .*

"The story of a Pioneer: Diana Wright's story of resilience and reinvention expose and present the depth of human experience. Her journey from maligned child to triumphant executive is a compelling story worth immersing yourself into."
  —Judy Reagan, Entrepreneur and Corporate Executive


"A rich and intriguing story of a brilliant woman's journey to self discovery. This book is exciting and suspenseful, giving hope to all those struggling to find themselves. And it's an excellent read ."
  —Barbara Bennett, Ph.d, Editor and Publishing Consultant


"This book is great for men to have insight into the female psyche."
  — Gary Farmer, Actor, Director


"A fascinating read . . . in this beautiful sometimes cruel and yet caring world that we live in."
  — Jay Tailor, BVM Medical LTD

# Too Damn Dumb To Think

# Too Damn Dumb To Think

DIANA WRIGHT WITH DR. BERNIE DECOKE

*Bink Books*
Bedazzled Ink Publishing Company • Fairfield, California

978-1-945805-97-4 paperback

Cover Design
by
Krista Moya

Front Cover Photographs
Krista Moya

Back Cover Photograph
Dr. Bernie DeCoke

Bink Books
a division of
Bedazzled Ink Publishing, LLC
Fairfield, California
http://www.bedazzledink.com

# Acknowledgements

*First, from Diana personally:*

To the love of my life for over 25 years, Dr. Bernie DeCoke. I thank you, my devoted partner, for all that you are and all that you do.

*Second, from the two of us:*

To our daughter, Paula, who died of cancer at 45 years of age. The foster care system needed you and you were there. You touched so many lives. We truly miss you.

To Dr. Christopher Lieu, Associate Professor at the University of Colorado. You professionally tended to our daughter's cancer treatment. Thank you for the compassion and loving support with which you treated the three of us. We will always be grateful and honored to call you friend.

To Fran Hart, Diana's sister, you so willingly shared memories, views and love.

To our longtime friends Betty Johnson and Lorrie Wright. We cherish you.

To our community, neighbors and friends—especially Jim and Jollene Peters, David Gave, Sr. (Paula and the character Ben's father), Wally and Nancy Gough, Karen and Dick Wehrman, Judy Reagan, Jia Apple and Mary Bolejack. Your acceptance of us and warm generosity makes our life rich.

To Claudia and Casey of Bedazzled Ink Publishing. You recognized the potential of our writing and this story. Your acceptance letter, initial confidence and encouragement spurred us on through all of the challenges.

To Leslie Wainger, who guided us in the right direction chapter by chapter.

To Barbara Bennet, PhD., who gave us a highly polished final manuscript.

To Kristi Moya. After Bernie and I worked together on this book for 16 years, by some miracle you came into our lives and into our writing process. With your work ethic, professional grace, sensitivity, respect, screen writing and graphic design experience, you were able to work harmoniously with us on the many aspects necessary to produce this book. Thank you and may your next film-directing opportunity come to fruition. Perhaps with this story.

# PROLOGUE

## A REFLECTION ON MY CHILDHOOD

THE WIND HOWLS. My bedroom window is glazed with ice. I dread crawling out of my warm bed every day at 4 o'clock in the morning. Groping for my heavy socks, stashed under the covers to warm up to get ready for the icy air, I shiver while quickly dressing in thermal underwear, jeans and a long-sleeved shirt. I tiptoe down the wooden stairs and feel heat coming up from the monster furnace that almost fills the basement of our old farmhouse. Usually when I get up the house is freezing, but today someone has stoked the furnace. The light is on in the kitchen. I see my mother in her food-smudged apron printed with quacking ducks. She's bending over the Sunday paper, which is spread open on the kitchen table.

I move across the floor and stare at the picture of my dad in his best shirt. The headline underneath says:

### WAYSIDE PARK NAMED IN HONOR OF
### PRESTIGIOUS 4-H LEADER

He's not my real dad. I was born after my mother had an affair with a married man in Canada. We then moved to the US where she married the man I have to call Dad.

"Aren't you proud?" Mother asked me.

"Uh huh," I said without looking up.

My stomach heaves. The article says he is generous and kind, he has created a market at local resorts for the fresh fryer chickens we raise and he donates hours of community service teaching children in 4-H how to make birdhouses and pig-shaped breadboards. This is not the father I know.

My eight-year-old brother and I have to milk 40 head of cattle, knock down hay from the loft, fill the feed troughs, shovel the dirty hay into a wheelbarrow, dump it on the manure pile, and feed and water the chickens—all before breakfast. Dad calls us the "outdoor shitheads." Our three younger sisters never have to help with chores; they are supposedly too young. In the summer Dad allows us time to work on our 4-H projects for the county fair; it's important to him that we win. It's the only time I ever hear him say anything good about us.

Mother ignores my silence and asks, "Do you want to help make oatmeal cookies, Diana?"

I look around the room and ask, "Me?"

"There's no one else here, is there?"

"No." I am shocked that my mother is asking me to bake with her, and I quickly say, "Yes, I want to."

I am 12 years old and long for a day with my mother. She is the breadwinner of the family and goes to work all week.

"Well, go fetch flour, sugar, and oatmeal."

I hurry to the tiny pantry with the tall ceiling. I imagine the taste of the sweet, freshly-baked cookies and my mouth waters. I read the labels on the shelves. I want to get it right.

Suddenly the porch door opens and bangs into the kitchen wall. I hear my stepfather shout, "Where the hell is Diana?" I back against the glass canning jars stored on the shelves, which make a clanking noise. I wait, hoping he hasn't heard.

"I thought she could help me bake this morning," Mother answers.

"You thought?" he yells. "Woman, you're too damn dumb to think. That's why I do all the thinking around here."

He comes to the pantry door, pointing the long stick he carries at me. "Get your fucking no-good brother up and get out to the barn. There's work to do."

I start toward the stairs. He takes a step toward me.

"Move or I'll beat you until you can't walk."

I race up the stairs and bang on my brother's door. I hear my mother start to argue. "Diana never gets to do anything inside."

He shouts his usual threats. "If you don't like it, move out. I couldn't give a goddamn."

Mother won't easily back down from him. Insults and threats will explode between them like firecrackers.

My brother and I help Dad herd the cows into the barn for milking.

"Shit outside, you son of a bitches." Dad hits old Betsy, the lead cow, with a board, roaring, "Don't shit on my clean barn floor." He smacks her again.

I hate to hear her loud moans, but I can't protect her. He is bigger and stronger and I'm afraid he will turn on me. Betsy's cries are like my own. Later I'll speak kind words and try to treat her bruises as best I can, but there is no one to protect any of us from my stepfather.

School gets me away from chores and the clutches of my stepfather. In addition to learning the usual subjects, we study Family Life and Sex Education, taught by the school nurse. One day I start to tremble in class. She notices and asks me what's wrong. I'm too afraid to say. She regards me for a moment, then sends me to her office. I try not to look at anyone when I leave the classroom. I hold my breath so I won't burst into tears.

When the nurse comes to her office she asks, "Diana, did something I say upset you?"

I'm scared and don't know what to tell her. Silent tears run down my face. She waits, then turns to take a kettle from a hot plate and pour steaming water into a pretty teapot.

I blurt, "My dad says it's his job to train me about sex." I try to see her face. It seems as though she is wearing a mask, her mouth held in a tight line.

She hands me one of the empty teacups that match the teapot. "Diana, I want you to throw this on the floor."

"I can't."

"It will help you feel better."

"It's too pretty."

"It's not important to me, but you are."

Always obedient, I take the cup and throw it on the floor. It breaks into tiny pieces. My whole body feels as though it has exploded, my legs give way and I fall backward into a chair.

"I have to report this to the sheriff," the nurse says. "Your dad should be arrested."

"No! It will ruin my family."

"I don't want to ruin your family. It's my job to keep you safe."

"I can deal with it."

"How?"

"I will talk to my stepfather and tell him if he touches me again, he will be arrested."

"Do you want me to come with you?"

"No."

She holds my gaze. My resolve doesn't waver. Finally, she says, "I must know that you are OK."

"After I have talked to him," I say, "I'll come and tell you."

"And if he touches you again?"

"You can call the sheriff."

He never touches me again.

# CHAPTER ONE

WHILE MY FIRST husband fought in Vietnam, I fought to prove my self-worth and intelligence. I fought to be in control of my life. The women of the sixties were waging a revolution that suited my own ambition perfectly.

I was a full time employee for Tasty Freeze and a part time student at CSU Fullerton. It took me nine years to get my bachelor's degree in Biological Science. Then the only job I could find was to hand sew pig-tissue heart valves for $6.50 an hour.

I got my younger sister a job when the company began to hire non-degreed employees. She boasted to the family that she was making as much as I was, without having to go to school for nine years. I kept the job even though it was torment to be humiliated by my family.

My perseverance paid off, and I was promoted to the engineering department a month later. My mother always said I was the most determined person she had ever known. I went on to engineer a new concept to modify the orifice of a heart valve. A tiny flap of pig tissue shaped my destiny. Many years later I became the founder, president, and CEO of Pioneering Entities, Inc., a company I started in Colorado that developed and manufactured custom medical devices.

I CONSIDERED THE agenda for the annual board meeting. It was concise and offered nothing requiring debate. I was determined not to repeat last year's meeting, when my second husband, William Wright, PhD, a brilliant design engineer and board member, schemed to take over the company.

During my career in heart valve engineering and during William's work inventing surgical products, we had made valuable contacts in the medical engineering field. But it was my vision that built Pioneering Entities from those connections.

I was proud of the company and felt good about its direction until last year's disastrous board meeting. Members of the board, which included William, insisted that more surgeons would want to bring us their new inventions to develop if the company had a more prestigious image. I argued that if we did expand, we should buy a property to offset liability by increasing the company's assets. The market was ready. It was obvious to me. However, my proposal was overruled because real estate investments were not considered to be within the company's purview. I was directed to lease a new facility. I was already so concerned about the financial stretch that I had taken no salary for the past year.

I saw that vote as an initial salvo to remove me, manipulated by my husband who lay coiled in wait to take over. William's aristocratic British ego allowed me no authority in any aspect of his life. I could be his princess but not the ruling queen.

I had lived with him long enough to be aware of his devious nature, but I had underestimated his ability to make board members believe he could run the company if they ousted me. In reality, he could never run it. He liked to play and develop products that never peaked in the marketplace, and we both knew it.

Impatiently I glanced at my watch, determined to hide my resentments. Today was to be the board's first visit to the new facility. I could hear voices in the reception area before I stepped into the hall. I walked carefully to soften the click of my heels on the floor as I approached. Paula, my 21-year-old daughter, was the office manager and receptionist. Her height gave her an authority her youth could not. She was very familiar with the current dynamics of the company. With professional ease she welcomed the board members as they arrived and offered refreshments. I grabbed Paula's hand and gave it a slight squeeze, to thank her for her role as I made my entrance.

"Good morning and welcome to our annual board meeting."

I looked at the board members, focusing on William. We had started out working in our kitchen, and now we had a 15,000 square-foot facility. The collaboration of his technical genius with my mechanical engineering aptitude and unstoppable determination birthed numerous medical device patents. Now I had to battle for my seat at the helm. How had I allowed my company to be governed by others?

I ushered the group into the meeting room after they toured the new facility. All eyes scanned the gunmetal-blue walls, plush silver-blue carpet, expansive walnut conference table surrounded by 16 chairs and the wall of wood-framed windows. It was a long way from my Minnesota farm-girl upbringing. The board members praised the elegant surroundings as they settled into chairs. I called the meeting to order and summed up the year's accomplishments. Pioneering Entities had made good progress, yet while sales were up the cash-flow dilemma and ongoing crisis to meet payroll never ended. I concluded with, "Lynn will prepare the minutes and send you a copy. Thank you all for coming."

I took my first deep breath. I looked over at Lynn, my Quality Assurance Manager, her hair swept back as she looked up from her notes and met my eyes with a slight grin. I liked this woman. She darted about the company, ensuring that all efforts resulted in a quality product. She had worked for me for three years, was my springboard for company issues and my confidante.

Several months earlier I had planned a camping and hiking trip in the Rocky Mountains. I knew that I would need to take a break from the stress of the company and my strained relationship with William. I invited Lynn to join me. She wasn't afraid to challenge me. I recalled our last racquetball game when she'd knocked me to the ground with her aggressive play. I smiled back at her. We planned to leave once the board meeting ended.

William, fourteen years my senior, his face alcohol blotched with bags under his gray eyes, stood, neatening up his finely woven black suit and silk tie. "Diana," he said in his British accent, "I must speak with you in my office." Before I could reply, he turned toward the board members and began to chat with them as they left the conference room. I exchanged a glance with Lynn, then moved toward the door to give and receive polite handshakes.

When only Lynn and I remained in the room, she asked, "Do you really think it's necessary to meet with William?"

"I wish I could avoid him but yes, it's necessary." Our eyes met. My heart pounded faster as I sensed a warm tenderness from her.

"Don't let him harass you," she said. "Remember we're trying to beat the rush hour traffic."

I nodded and walked toward William's office. The hallway, lined with oak-framed patents of company-owned products, seemed longer than usual. Paula intercepted me with my cocker spaniel puppy, Parker, in her arms.

"Mom, how did it go?" she asked. "Are you OK?"

I scratched under Parker's chin. "I'm exhausted but it's over. You were wonderful. I'm so proud of you and grateful for all that you do. I wasn't challenged by anyone and I bought more time to steady the company."

Paula knew the previous board meeting had been a gang attack, a derailing of each business proposal I had offered. It had traumatized her nearly as much as it did me.

"William wants a minute before I leave with Lynn."

"Mom, you don't have to take his shit. I don't know why you tread so lightly with him."

"I have too much at stake right now."

"You're too generous." Then, "I'll walk Parker so she's ready to go."

I smiled. "Thank you, sweetheart."

Parker stayed tucked away in Paula's office during the work day. William had given her to me. He said she was a gift, but I saw it as a tactic to force me to come home. He was well aware that my newly leased apartment didn't allow pets. I loved our ranch and the animals. It was another loss for me when I left him.

I knew when I entered his office that he was ready to attack. I could smell his dank perspiration mingled with his cologne. My nose twitched. I stepped over the numerous projects on the floor.

William began his assault mildly. "You're really going on a holiday without me?"

"We've talked this to death. Do you have any questions about what needs to be done while I'm gone?"

His face reddened. "First you get your own flat which is unnecessary and blimey embarrassing."

"I won't let you hurt my kids."

"I didn't hurt Ben," he said, referring to my son, his stepson, who was 17, four years younger than Paula.

"You tried to choke him."

"He was late and disrespectful."

"Your behavior was shameful."

He gripped the edge of his desk and through clenched jaws he said, "I'm still your husband, Diana. You should be home, not in some fool flat, or going on holiday with Lynn. I'm stuck with all of your damn animals."

"That was your choice. You want the apartment?"

"Hell no, I want you."

"You've had your chance. First you wouldn't hear of counseling. Then you'd only go if you selected the therapist, and after one session you claimed he didn't know what he was talking about."

"He didn't. A bloody idiot he was."

"I don't want to fight with you anymore."

"Let's sort this out together on this trip."

"You're the reason I need to get away."

I stopped before I revealed my knowledge of his attempts to coerce the board to remove me and install him as CEO. I was still forming my strategy to regain control of the company and end our marriage.

He looked down and when he lifted his head his tactics changed from an angry attack to malicious innuendo. "It seems a bad choice for the president and the quality assurance manager to go missing at the same time."

"It's only two workdays. We'll be back on Monday. You're upper management; you can deal with it."

But I knew William couldn't deal with it. Was I being sensible? No. Was this trip necessary? Yes.

William started to come around his desk. "Dick's a lazy sod. He lets Lynn do whatever she wants."

"Lynn's husband was also not invited, but unlike you he's fine with it." I headed for the door, saying, "You should thank him. It was his idea to have a picnic on Sunday instead of just taking us back to the trailhead to pick up the jeep. You can meet us or not, your choice."

I walked away. Once out of sight of William, I tipped my head upward so my tears didn't smear my mascara. I licked my lips, tasting salty frustration, then ran my tongue over my slightly protruding front teeth. My body trembled. I ducked into the restroom, grateful I didn't meet anyone, and slumped over the sink. It wasn't like this in the beginning.

I met William when I was employed as an engineering tech at Beagerton Medical Devices Inc. He was the well-known, world-traveled engineer. Flattered as I was that a man of his position and intelligence showed an interest in me, the failure of my first marriage filled me with trepidation. In the 18 months we dated, William showered me with jewelry, fine clothes, and romantic dinners. He took Paula, Ben, and I to private openings at museums and sightseeing trips along the coast. One time he suggested that we all fly to New York to see the smash Broadway play, *Napoleon,* but then he said he couldn't get tickets. I found out later that he was completely in debt.

Our family was happy for the first two years out of our ten-year marriage. Paula and Ben had expensive clothes. They were able to join after-school clubs and make new friends. My former single-parent guilt was soothed. William's high-paying career allowed me to relax and feel pampered by his attention. I still worked full time, so we took turns cooking gourmet dinners, always romantic with candlelight and special wines. Every other weekend he took me on long drives while the radio blared from his Mazda RX7 and we sang along with the songs we loved.

Then it seemed to melt away like butter on a hot summer day. William closed himself in his workshop to endlessly toy with the rebuilding of a vintage sports car. He had always been a heavy drinker, but it radically increased. I was shelved away to be used for occasional sex and when he needed clean socks. The children had school, friends, and chores to keep them occupied.

I turned my disillusion and pain into a determination to fulfill my dream and form my own company. I networked with business lawyers, corporate executives, and investors. My business plan was completed, then altered with directions changed as investors were finalized. Each new contact or prospective client was an asset. Every new product represented a possibility for long-term profits. William scoffed but I persevered and Pioneering Entities Inc. was launched in 1987. The hurt I felt from William's detachment faded. I had my children and a dream finally come true. I had my own company.

A year later when William was faced with a choice of relocating to the East Coast or losing his job, he quit. "Idiots, the lot of 'em," he said. "I'm not working on that bloomin' project one more minute." He became more reclusive as months went by and his employment opportunities dwindled.

I began to consider hiring William, as his innovative design concepts could benefit my new company. We needed a product

line. He had been an associate professor at Liverpool University
and had published papers in every medical journal. I didn't
have his credentials. He would bring ballast to the company.
His previous employers had difficulty keeping him focused on
projects. He would veer off on personal tangents, but I knew his
weaknesses and he was still my husband. At the time I thought I
could manage him, but now he was plotting to replace me.

I looked in the restroom mirror and saw exhaustion. I bathed
my face with water. I hurriedly took my dress and slip off,
wiping under my breasts and arms with dampened paper towels.
I peeled off my pantyhose like a snake shedding old skin and
dressed in a pale green long-sleeved shirt, wool socks, jeans, and
leather hiking boots. This time the mirror reflected a glimmer of
victory in my tired eyes. I was ready to let the Rocky Mountain
wilderness restore me.

When I walked into my office, Lynn was looking at the
framed article, *The Story of a Pioneer*, that featured me on the
cover, published in an executive medical device magazine. That
photo shoot took four hours—three were just for makeup. My
shoulder-length brown curly hair was so coated with hairspray
that not a strand moved in the wake of the fan. The breeze was
meant to eliminate perspiration tracking through the makeup
that covered the stress lines of a forty-five-year-old woman. It
was the first time the reddish birthmark at the crown of my nose
wasn't apparent. A mauve lipstick was used to widen my thin
lips. The image looked better than the real deal.

Lynn was dressed in patched jeans, a faded plaid flannel shirt,
and scuffed-up leather hiking boots. She turned to me and said,
"How was William?"

I closed the door behind me. "Typical. Let's talk about it
later." I walked to my desk, draped my dress over the chair.
"You're sure you're OK with this?"

"Of course!" Lynn exclaimed.

Lynn was raised as a Roman Catholic in the Midwest and
was a few years older than me. She had worked most of her life,

married her one and only sweetheart, and rapidly had two sons. I found it easy to tell her my thoughts and feelings; but the more I shared, the more vulnerable I felt. My intuitive receptors didn't seem to be able to read her the way I usually read people. Would a deepening friendship change our ability to work together? And then there were those twinges I felt but couldn't explain, even to myself. For me everything about this friendship was complex, unorthodox, disturbing, and exhilarating.

"Did you bring wine?" she asked.

"Yes. A merlot carefully wrapped in my pack."

"Then let's get out of here, shall we?"

I nodded, and we walked out to the hall. I was locking my office door when we heard the patter of puppy feet. Parker jumped and circled me happily. I scratched her head and saw Paula at the end of the hall.

Though we'd experienced some less than harmonious times, Paula and I loved each other, and my employees knew we shared a bond not to be tested. Paula diligently looked after everyone and everything she cared about. She severed the relationship she had with her stepfather, William, when his maniacal rule threatened us. Paula, Lynn, and I walked to the parking lot with Parker vying for my attention. I noticed Paula's baby bump and gently patted her mini-mound.

She smiled. "Not too excited about being a grandmother, are you, Mom?"

"I'm still getting used to the idea, but I'm thrilled," I said. "Give me another five months and I'll be as ready as you are."

"You think I'll be ready?" She stopped in front of me.

"You'll be a great mother."

"I've always wanted to be a mother," she said. "But?"

"It's perfectly normal to be nervous, especially during your first pregnancy. You haven't had any reasons for concern. Why the apprehension?"

"It's not having a baby or becoming a mother. It's being a wife."

"I didn't know you planned on getting married," I said, startled.

Paula and I talked all the time and this was her first mention of marriage. Parker brushed our legs with her body as she zipped around us.

"I wasn't, but with the baby coming." Paula looked at me, confusion in her eyes.

"Diana, it's getting late, and you hoped to beat the rush hour traffic," Lynn said.

"I'll be right there."

"I know you want this baby," I said, opening the trunk of my car. "But do you want to get married?"

"Oh, Mom, it's OK. I'm not eloping this minute. For heaven's sake, we haven't even tried living together."

I searched for the right words while Paula grabbed my pack, gloves, and parka. We carried them over to Lynn's jeep.

"You don't have to get married. I mean, I'll help with the baby."

"I know."

I loaded Parker in the back seat, then turned to Paula. Her wavy brown hair swept back from her forehead and her crystal-clear blue eyes were shadowed by thick brows. I had no doubt the baby's father loved my daughter. But had he won her love?

"I'd never get married without you, Mom."

"Promise?" I said.

"Of course!"

I wrapped my arms tightly around her.

"Take care, Mom," Paula whispered. "Everything will be fine."

"We'll talk lots when I get back. I love you."

"I know, Mom, me too."

"Take care," she said politely to Lynn.

Paula was not fond of Lynn, but she was not an athletic person and most definitely would not subject herself to the blisters or body aches of a hiking trip. She would prefer volunteering at the Humane Society to care for abandoned animals.

"Goodbye, Paula," Lynn said. "I know everything is in good hands."

"Why wouldn't it be?" Paula shot back.

Lynn held her keys out to me. She knew how much I loved to drive a rugged vehicle. I slid behind the steering wheel and waved to Paula as we pulled away.

# CHAPTER TWO

I BACKED LYNN'S jeep out carefully. The leather-wrapped steering wheel had a nice feel. The jeep responded to the gentlest touch. I could feel the stiff springs when we hit the first bump in the road. My desire to speed away and get there was bridled by the traffic lights.

"Your knuckles are white," Lynn said. "Do you think it might help to loosen your grip?"

I uncurled and stretched my fingers. several repetitions were necessary.

She watched me. "Since you're driving I'll be navigator."

"Like when we play racquetball and you make me run all over the court?"

"I confess, it gives me a thrill to beat you at something."

"Me, too," I said. "I mean I like the competition, but I don't like to get beaten."

"That's obvious!" She laughed. "But you're a good sport and you keep coming back to play."

Racquetball was my stress reliever. I would imagine someone when I hit the ball, and the resounding whack gave me satisfaction. I also enjoyed the collisions with Lynn on the court. I experienced a thrill that had nothing to do with the game.

The road ran wide and straight through rocky, sage-covered foothills that rose on both sides. We crested a hill and saw the jagged indigo ridges of the distant peaks, a sharp contrast to the brilliant turquoise of the vast sky. I stretched in the seat, took a deep breath, and let out a full-throated scream. Lynn jumped, stared at me with her mouth agape, then gave her own ear-splitting yell. We looked at each other in shock and burst out laughing. I noticed the contours of her breasts, showing faintly under the flannel shirt. I hoped she couldn't read my thoughts. I was middle aged and had not felt this intense desire for a woman before and never for a man. She's an employee, I told myself. I knew that when I planned this trip, but I invited her anyway, driven to explore and find answers to the feelings within me.

"Would you like to listen to some music?" Lynn asked.

"Sure." Her question brought me back from my thoughts.

"What do you listen to?"

"Driving is my quiet time to review and strategize."

"You never stop working, do you?"

"If I did none of us would have jobs."

"What made you take the time for this trip?"

"I feel like a pressure cooker ready to explode. I don't want to do something stupid that could jeopardize everything I've built. A strenuous hike in the wilderness will help me blow off some steam."

"Why did you ask me to spend such precious time with you?"

I paused to decide how much to reveal in my answer. "I'm surrounded by people who either depend on me or want to overrule me. I don't feel that with you."

Lynn smiled. "Will you trust my music choice then?"

I laughed. "It's your serve!"

Lynn reached into her purse and pulled out two tapes. "I brought Yanni and Enya." She held them up. "Which do you prefer?"

"That's a hard choice. I don't know either of them."

She laughed. "Let's listen to Yanni first. Dick and I have tickets to hear him at the Red Rocks Amphitheater. We can pretend we're at the concert. I wish you were going with me instead of Dick."

She and Dick had two teenage boys and appeared to have a good relationship. They frequently went on family trips. Her comment was curious. I felt pleased and baffled at the same time.

Lynn loaded the tape into the player. I let the harmonious Yanni be the music score to my mental rollercoaster. My emotions leapt in excitement when Lynn touched my leg, fell when she mentioned Dick, then rose again when she talked as if there was a possible us. Her touch sent a tingling sensation through me, and I squeezed my thighs together to focus on the road. Here I am, dauntless entrepreneur Diana Wright, in a froth because I can't admit to myself the feelings I have for this woman. Several years before, a business partner admitted to me that she was a lesbian and had wondered if that would be a problem for me. I said her choice was not a problem as long as she understood that I was not. At the time I had no idea the struggle she must have gone through to tell me. But I did now and I hated it. I opened the window to let the cool air refresh me.

"What do you think?" Lynn asked.

"About what?" I asked.

"The music. Do you like Yanni?"

"It's soothing," I answered.

The music did not disturb my thoughts, as I kept digging for insight into how Lynn felt about me and how she would react if I revealed my true feelings toward her. I was shocked to feel jealous of her husband just because he was going to the concert with her. She always spoke respectfully of him. He worked for a cable company, had a good position, adequate income, and was close to retirement.

I closed the window to hear the music better. I needed to stop my jumble of thoughts. When the song ended I asked, "Navigator, how much longer? Will we arrive early enough to set up camp before dark?"

"We might need to park at the trailhead and sleep in the jeep for the night."

"That would work. Are you hungry?"

"Nope."

"Lynn, you're never hungry. I need food."

"I know of a restaurant up ahead."

I grinned and poked her side gently. "How many times have you hiked this trail?"

She tipped toward me and giggled. "Dick and I come up here with the boys sometimes." She grabbed my hand. "I'm ticklish. The restaurant is in the next town." She let go of my hand.

I was disappointed that she dropped my hand, and I felt the same pang of jealousy. A click sounded and the music stopped. Lynn reached over to change the tape.

"Lynn," I said, "I've got to ask you something."

She looked at me, the next tape in her hand, and waited.

"Do you think William has a chance to sway the board to support his takeover attempt? Can I divorce him and not undermine my position?"

She stared at me. "Are you serious?"

"Very."

"I'm a shareholder and your friend. I believe in Pioneering because I believe in you. William is a genius at developing product, but is working with him worth the emotional toll?"

"He was so considerate and loving when we met; I don't understand what changed him. How could I have been so wrong?" I shook my head.

"I think the question you have to answer is what will happen to Pioneering if you crumble under his machinations?"

I stopped breathing and tightened my grip on the wheel. That was the blunt, right-in-your-face Lynn who kept staff producing the quality surgical devices required in our business.

"You take care of everyone and everything except yourself. You care too much about not being a failure." She was right. I couldn't fail. Ever.

Yet here I was dealing with another failed marriage. William had become a madman who hated the world. The image of him naked and so raging drunk that he was falling into walls haunted me. One night his fury turned into a violent fight with Ben. William had never laid a hand on me or my children before. His assaults were always verbal. I was able to get out of the house with Ben, and we moved the very next day. Now I just had to figure out how to extricate him from the company.

When I launched Pioneering, I thought I finally had my destiny in my own hands. But an under-financed startup requires investors, and they need assurances. The compromises you have to make can whittle away your power.

I loosened my grip on the steering wheel and forced a tight smile. "Let's hear the other tape."

Lynn hit the play button and Enya, soft and ethereal, flowed into the jeep. She placed her hand on my neck. "Your neck's really rigid."

"Yes," I said, hoping she didn't notice how her unexpected touch made me even more taut. Her hands were warm as she ran her fingers along my neck and down my shoulder.

"That feels wonderful," I said, encouraging her not to stop.

"What are you going to do about William?" she said, jolting me back to a far less desirable place. "You're avoiding the subject. You always do."

"Do I?" I knew full well she was right. Sometimes it was a conscious tactic. Other times it was just my brain flitting faster than the conversation.

"Well, what are you going to do?"

"I know what I want to do, but it's complicated. The board thinks the management team is fragile. They're watching carefully."

"You're masterful at handling William," Lynn said in a soft tone. "You'll figure it out. Let me know if I can help."

"You and Dick seem very comfortable with each other." Secretly I thought he was a bore.

"Oh, we've had our problems. He rules the boys with an iron hand, and I haven't been able to soften him. He's the man of the family. I accept that. It's safer for all of us."

"Safer?" I asked. "What does safer mean?"

"I want to be sure about my future." Lynn looked out the window. The sunset cast long shadows. "Didn't you leave William for your safety and Ben's?"

I nodded. "I tried to protect my son for a long time, first from his biological father and then from William. He adored William. His birth father has always ignored him. After that awful fight, Ben's admiration for William turned to disgust. It's changed him, and I'm not quite sure how."

"So you agree, safe is not a bad thing."

"Maybe, but isn't there more to an intimate relationship? What about mutual respect, spiritual growth, intellectual stimulation and joy?"

"You're a romantic! Look around you, Diana. People are lucky to have any joy at all. Life for most of us demands hard and steady work."

"I'm not afraid of hard work, as you well know."

"Survival is better than the alternative."

"Are you and Dick just about survival?"

"We're no dynamic duo, but we work well together and I know what to expect." Lynn paused. "He's pleasant company."

"I want more than routine drudgery and pleasant company."

"Well, Diana, you want a lot. Most of us start out dreaming of more, but it's not what we find. I personally doubt that more is possible unless you're rich." Lynn grinned at me. "If more is what you're going for, it would help if you started taking a paycheck."

I smiled back at her. "Good idea."

Rounding a curve, we saw a few buildings and a restaurant sign.

"Is this our food stop?" I asked, hopefully.

Lynn nodded. "This is the place I told you about."

I pulled the jeep into the parking lot. Parker jumped out almost before I got the leash attached, nosed around, and dashed into some weeds. She squatted next to a clump of wild columbines and stopped when the prickly stems hit her belly. Then she spun, pawed, lowered her rear, and peed. I walked her back to the jeep.

Lynn and I went inside the rustic cafe. Deer, elk, and antlered rabbit heads, called jackalopes, were mounted on the walls.

Their sightless eyes felt like surveillance cameras. We passed wood-plank tables and thick oak chairs with hollowed-out seats, made either by design or by years of use. At the counter, we placed our to-go order of elk burgers and hand cut fries.

I paid and we walked back to the jeep. I held up the keys. "Do you want to drive?"

"Go ahead," she said, "if you want to."

"OK," I said, feeling lighthearted and chivalrous.

I walked Lynn to the passenger side, unlocked, and opened the door for her. Parker poked her nose up from the back, sniffing the bags. When Lynn was seated with the food safely tucked between her feet on the floor, I took her hand between mine. "Thank you for listening. I appreciate your friendship so much."

She smiled and squeezed my hand. I walked around to the driver's seat, enjoying the warmth that radiated up my arms.

Lynn carefully rewrapped my burger for one-handed eating. I maneuvered back onto the road. We shared several morsels with Parker, who noisily chomped her share. I ate my meal, savoring the simple food.

"You have ketchup on your chin." Lynn wiped it off with a napkin.

"Thanks," I said, surprised.

She grinned. "Quality assurance manager, at your service!"

I laughed. "I enjoy good bread. The bun tasted freshly baked like my mother's yeast rolls."

"Food is fuel for me," Lynn said. "I don't care too much about what I eat, as long as it's nutritious."

Suddenly the paved road turned to gravel and the washboard made the jeep vibrate.

Lynn grabbed the door handle tightly. "Would you please slow down? It's 19 miles of this all the way to the campground. I would hate to break an axle and have to call Dick to come and get us."

I slowed down.

Thirty minutes later the dust had permeated the jeep, and Parker sneezed.

When the headlights flashed on the campground sign, Lynn said, "I think I'm going to be sick." She put her hand to her forehead, the center of her chest, then both shoulders. "Thank you, God! We got here alive."

"I was going slowly."

"Really?"

"I thought I was," I said as I pulled into the parking lot. "There are no campers in sight."

"It's Thursday." Lynn said. "Too early for the weekend crowds."

I peered at her in the dusty interior. "Are you all right?"

She nodded.

I opened the door and Parker bounded out and ran. She scurried about, nose to the ground. When she bumped into a tree she looked toward a rustle of leaves and the chatter from a disgruntled squirrel. Parker responded with several yips. I allowed this conversation to go on for a short time, until they began to sound like William and me.

Lynn and I fluffed our sleeping bags in the front seats. I helped Parker settle into her place in the back. Lynn moved to the driver's side to give my longer legs extra room. We snuggled in as best we could.

"Do you believe how cold it is already?" Lynn said through clenched teeth as she arranged the bag around her.

"You're freezing because you're so skinny. We could run the engine and turn the heater on for a little while if you want."

"No, I'll warm up. I'll be fine."

Lynn would forgo comfort to save money. She saved so she could enjoy life later. I didn't believe I had a long future. My parents both died young. I live for right now.

In the dark I smiled. "We'll get an early start tomorrow." I stopped talking after I heard Lynn's soft snore. I whispered into the velvety night, "I'm here. I'm really doing this." I hoped for magic to happen in my life once again.

# CHAPTER THREE

THE LESS THAN ideal sleeping quarters required numerous position adjustments throughout the night. I was grateful for daybreak. The car windows were fogged from our overnight breathing. As I peered through the blurry windshield, I saw big round eyes and a dark charcoal nose over the jeep hood. Straining, I could make out five points on each of his antlers.

Lynn stirred.

In a hushed, calm voice I whispered, "Don't move. Do you see the buck?"

Suddenly Parker barked and leapt toward the front window, hairs standing erect along her spine. I shot to the roof. The buck bounded into the woods. Lynn bolted upright and wrapped herself around the steering wheel. I tried to pull the excited puppy from the dashboard. Lynn shot me a dirty look.

I struggled to contain Parker on my lap and rubbed my head checking for any damage. "Good morning."

"Big attitude for such a little dog," she retorted. Then down went the zipper and out of the sleeping bag and jeep she went.

There was no one at the campsites or parking area. I let Parker out to run and did a few stretches to lessen the aches from sleeping contorted in the passenger seat. The early morning sky was marbled with shades of pink, gold, and blue. The dark green needles on the pine trees complemented the golden-orange leaves of the aspen trees in the pale light of dawn. My heightened senses took in the palette of colors and crisp fragrances of sunrise in the mountains.

"Do you want coffee and breakfast?" Lynn asked.

"I would if it weren't so cold. Let's get to our campsite so we can build a lovely fire and enjoy all this beauty without shivering."

"How hard did you bump your head?" Lynn asked. "I've never known you to be so poetic."

I laughed. "Maybe someday I'll be a writer."

We strapped the rolled sleeping bags back onto our packs and pulled them upright on the tailgate. We slid our arms into the straps and tightened the waistbands. I inhaled the crisp, fresh mountain air. My lungs swelled. I felt lightheaded and eager to get on the path.

The 46 pound pack seemed lighter and more maneuverable than the weight I carried as CEO of a struggling, undercapitalized corporation.

The gravel trail started out wide and spread even wider at the little creek. Parker put her head in the water, shook it, and sneezed. I tried to coax her to cross with us on the small wooden walkway, but she pawed at the water, took a step, and then bounded across. She looked back, her eyes like huge marbles, her head high, chest prominent, and her feet squarely set in a perfectly executed show stance. Parker's energetic and inquisitive nature matched mine perfectly.

Lynn and I exchanged broad smiles that broke into snickers over the pup's antics.

"This is it," she said softly, her eyes sparkling. "You and I. We're finally here."

I picked up a colorful leaf from the side of the path. It was wet. My fingers followed the center vein to the pointed tip. It bent easily from the pressure. I held it up. "Isn't it beautiful? This is real. I can smell it. I can touch it."

"Yes. I don't think I've ever seen a prettier autumn in Colorado."

"Did you notice the bushes and the grasses? Sometimes I think their autumn hues are even more magnificent than the trees."

Parker dashed past us, veered off the dirt path, and raced through the gently waving purples, yellows, and reds of the grasses.

Lynn looked at me with a smile. "You notice everything, don't you?"

"What do you mean?"

"I notice the scenery. You see the detail of each leaf."

"Stop. Close your eyes."

Obediently, Lynn closed her eyes. "Why?"

"I want to show you something."

She opened her eyes. "How can I see if I close my eyes?"

I laughed. "Trust me."

Lynn closed her eyes again. "I know better than to trust someone who says that, but I do trust you."

"What do you hear?"

"You."

"No, no, no. Other than me."

Lynn was quiet. "Birds."

"Yes. What else?" I waited.

"I hear soft rattling and whooshing." Lynn's eyes popped open. Her pupils shrank in the brilliant sunlight.

She turned toward the sounds to check out her senses. "I've never noticed how the leaves and grasses hum when the wind blows through them. It's incredible."

Her smile made her rosy cheeks seem more radiant. Laugh lines flowed like delicate tributaries beside her eyes. A fringe of light brown and gray curly bangs peeked out from beneath her ski cap. I watched her and felt my own delight intensify.

"You won't hear that in a board meeting," I said.

"No, but you do hear a lot of hot air."

We traveled a fair distance by lunchtime. My spirits were soaring but I was tired. Lynn's energy seemed unaffected by the journey or the weight of her pack. Her stamina invigorated me.

Our sights were set on camping at the intersection of Pawnee Creek and Thunderbolt Trails. Pushing on at a steady pace, we'd be there a little before dusk. The trail narrowed, winding through stands of aspen, spruce, juniper, and pine, their scents strong as our packs brushed against their branches. I paused to enjoy another deep breath and savor the fragrance, when a wave of dizziness staggered me.

"Are you all right?" Lynn asked as she pulled up behind me.

"Yes, I think so. A little light headed from trying to breathe in the forest. I guess my lungs aren't used to such a rush."

"Could be the thinner air at this altitude."

"Yes, and the lack of pollution."

My balance returned and I started up the rock-strewn dirt path. Lynn followed closely behind. Parker was several feet ahead, nose to the ground.

"Thank you for joining me out here," I said.

"I wouldn't have missed it."

"William certainly didn't like me going without him."

"He wants you there and here you are with me."

"Was it difficult for you to get away?"

"Dick didn't like that it was just you and me. He said he was worried about us out here alone. Maybe it's a guy thing."

"A guy thing?"

"A combination of jealousy, protectiveness, and control."

I pushed her. "Doesn't that feel like domination to you?"

"It's just the female and male aspects of nature. You learn to live with it."

"So how did you settle it with Dick?" I held back a pine bough to keep it from slapping Lynn in the face.

"I said if he wants to feel included he can bring a picnic lunch when he comes to give us a ride back to the jeep on Sunday," she said.

Surprised at her ingenuity, I looked at her behind me. "That was your idea?" Suddenly I tripped and tumbled backward onto my pack. Parker ran to check out the situation.

"Are you OK?" Lynn asked.

"I'm fine, soft landing."

Lynn kept her face and tone serious. "One of the basic rules about hiking is always to watch where you're going." Then she let out a giggle and extended her arm to assist me.

The additional weight of my pack pulled her down on top of me. We lay together sandwiched between the packs. A surge of electricity ripped through my body. Lynn laughed and clumsily rolled off me. A quiver shot through my chest and legs. Her soft body didn't feel heavy. It felt more like a comforter, warm and consoling. When we started walking again I felt lighter, as though a pressure that held me down had been lifted.

"Guess I don't need to ask if you're all right," Lynn said.

I laughed. "Am I going too fast?"

"Faster than you've been going."

It was true. "You tired, Lynn?"

"A little."

"I know what you need."

"What?"

"A warm fire. A little wine. Oh shit! The wine." I foolishly turned in a circle, trying to check the pack on my back. "Is anything leaking?"

Lynn followed me around once before pulling me to a stop. "If you'd stop turning, I could look." After a moment she announced, "I don't see anything leaking."

"Let's go then. It looks like we may have half an hour before sunset."

The path widened into a grassy meadow. A creek bordered one side. A large firepit was in the center surrounded by log seats. We had arrived at our first camp.

Grasshoppers rose up in flight. Parker leapt after them, playing a futile game of leapfrog until she lost interest and collapsed near the backpacks to doze. Lynn and I gathered wood, rebuilt the rock-lined fire ring, started a fire, pitched the tent, shook out the sleeping bags, and spread them out inside. We worked as if we were two beavers busily constructing a dam.

Our meal was canned stew, the heaviest food item in my pack. We had planned it for our dinner at the trailhead on our first night, but I ended up carrying it all those miles. We ate the stew from the can, paired with the wine, which we drank straight from the bottle. For dessert we each had an apple.

I drank water to temper my thirst between sips of wine. At this altitude the effects of the wine would hit quickly. Cleanup consisted of dipping two spoons in hot water and wiping them dry. The remainder of the stew was poured over Parker's dry dog food, which she thoroughly enjoyed. The charred empty can was placed in the trash bag we carried.

I added several hefty pieces of wood to the fire and grabbed the bottle of wine before I sat beside Lynn on the log seats. I held the bottle up. "To Friday night spent together in the wilderness."

She took the bottle from me. "To us." She took a swig then passed it back to me and turned to watch the fire. I took a sip and wondered if the flash of excitement that ran through me made the flames suddenly blaze, sending a fiery cloud of sparks into the black velvet sky.

"Out here there are more stars than sky," I said.

"There's no light glow from cities. Makes a difference."

"You make a difference to me." I looked at Lynn, the reflection of the fire making her eyes glow like amber.

She slid her hand onto my thigh. I glanced down and held her hand before she could take it away, although the magnetic pull generated by my body wouldn't have let her go.

"You're freezing," I said, then removed my gloves, careful not to lose hold of her, and slid my fingers over hers. She felt chilled. A tingle radiated through my leg.

After taking the last sip of wine, Lynn set the bottle down, placed her other hand on mine, and faced me. Our eyes met, and our warm breath in the cold air created a fog that made our connection seem mystical.

Had I lost my mind? I wanted to run. I never wanted to leave. I wanted more. I dared not ask.

Our gaze stayed locked, her face and lips only inches from mine. What I did next could affect me forever, perhaps repulse her or transform us. Her hand on my thigh was a sign. The first move would have to be from her, and would have to be crystal clear in order for me to risk everything. Had the wine made her bold? The seconds passed and she made no move. I imagined the sensation of her lips on mine. Temptation would win if I waited any longer. I glanced toward the fire pit. The flames had died. Ignoring my frustration, I pushed off from the log seat, finding that stiffness had crept over my muscles. Lynn was also slow to rise. If I read her correctly, she too was confused and disappointed. The moment had been lost.

"Kinda stiff. You?"

"Can hardly move."

We leaned on each other for support as we shuffled toward the tent. Once inside the snug two-person tent, Lynn closed the zipper and flaps. She turned on the flashlight and hung it from the center pole. I arranged the bedding. Before I'd finished Parker had wiggled into Lynn's bag.

We undressed and re-dressed for bed. The harder I tried to give her room, the more contact we seemed to make. When she hit her elbow in my ribs I laughed. She wrestled me down, tickling wherever there was an opening in my pajamas. I loved it. My heart leapt. I drew her to me. I started to kiss her neck but caught myself. I could feel the warmth of my exhale blow lightly back onto my face. Was this mind-shattering sexual desire that I felt just a friendly tussle for her? I needed her to kiss me. That was it. I couldn't initiate. She must. A kiss from her and I'd leap with her into the future.

But Lynn rose push-up style, above my body. She blocked the beam from the flashlight. I tried to see her face when a single drop of moisture fell on my neck. She rolled off and onto her back.

We lay quietly, side by side. Was it a tear that fell on me? Why had she turned away? Did she expect me to take charge? Is she scared of my rejection, afraid of the repercussions in her life, work, and family? Just like I was.

The scuffle had warmed us but then the cold temperature in the tent hit. We climbed into our sleeping bags. Lynn slithered into hers so as not to disturb Parker. Her contortions caused another bout of giggling, this time less boisterous.

"I haven't laughed like this in years," Lynn said as she turned off the light. "I'm so glad you planned this trip."

"Really?"

"Really!"

Our voices seemed loud in the quiet wilderness. Soon I heard Lynn's rhythmic snoring. I was thankful it was so dark in the tent. My passion would not fade. My heart was pounding. When we fell together on the floor of the racquetball court, I hadn't imagined it would lead to this. I wanted to touch, hold, and kiss a woman, a married woman, an employee. This went beyond midlife insanity. I lay rigid in my sleeping bag, not daring to move for fear of what I might do. I had shown a part of myself to Lynn that I hadn't known existed.

Had I been living a lie? Did my marriages fail because I could not love a man? Did the abuse I suffered from my stepfather turn my desires to a woman? Had my first attempt at intimacy with a woman just been rejected? I lay awake late into the night. Life as I had known it was over.

# CHAPTER FOUR

SATURDAY MORNING BROUGHT heavy condensation inside the tent, along with backpackers' aches and bewilderment. Lynn and I had just spent a night alone. Yet I awakened to another day where I had to guess at what this time together will bring.

"I'm cold. My bag's soaked," Lynn said as she started her dress-in-the-bag act.

"Wet? I'm not wet. The tent walls are wet but it shouldn't have any leaks. It is brand new," I said defensively.

"Well, my bag is wet." Lynn pulled both arms out of the bag. Her brows knotted as she blurted, "I don't believe it!"

"What?"

"Your dog. She peed. She peed in my bag."

"I'm so sorry," I said, trying to decide what I could do.

She snarled Parker's name as she kicked her way out of the offending bag.

I laughed. I shouldn't have, but I couldn't help it.

"Funny? You think it's funny? She's in your bag tonight."

Parker ran to me. I was touched by the sadness I saw in her eyes. She flicked her tongue across my nose. Lynn snatched up the bag and left the tent.

"Perhaps I shouldn't have laughed," I whispered to Parker as I stroked her head and ears.

Gone was the warm, lighthearted coziness of the previous evening. Had I gone too far, expected too much? I had known this might happen and thought it worth the risk. But I hadn't kissed her so she couldn't be sure. I'd considered the dangers of kissing this woman, but I'd failed to anticipate the consequences of not kissing her. How could I stand to be with Lynn for the rest of this trip? How could we work together?

I heard the snap of twigs, the scrape of a match, followed by a brief whiff of sulfur, then the crackle of a fire. My shoulder and back muscles ached. I stretched, trying to loosen them. Parker exited. The air was frigid, but it was time to leave the warm cocoon. Time to face the day and the woman over whom I anguished. I rolled over and struggled to get my knees under me. I found my legs numb and slow to respond. With my jaw set firm and despite the pain in my back, I moved out of the tent.

Lynn was standing directly in front of me when I stood.

"Coffee?" Lynn asked, offering me a steaming hot mug.

"Let me just sit down first. I'm a little . . ." I started and stopped. "I don't know what I am." My legs weren't right, they were numb. To be sore, tired, or even cramping would have been more rational. Weird as this was feeling, there had to be an explanation and I knew better than to tell Lynn and have her panic.

Lynn offered her free arm for me to steady myself. "What's wrong?" she asked and helped me to a place by the fire.

"I don't know. I feel really strange, sort of weak and exhausted. Guess I overdid it yesterday."

"But you're gonna be OK, right?"

"Yes of course." I knew I had to because this trip was about resolving issues, and so far they had compounded.

"You up for coffee?" Lynn asked, again offering the cup.

"Yes, it smells good. Thanks."

We sat and sipped coffee. Lynn had already started heating water over the fire, and when it boiled she added a packet of oatmeal. After she stirred, covered, and removed it from the heat, she sat back down and looked intently at me. "Well, your color's good. Your hands are steady. Are you hungry?"

"Yes."

"That's a good sign." She felt my forehead. "No fever, either. Hope oatmeal's OK."

"It's perfect," I replied.

Lynn removed the cover from the pot, slid it over to me, and handed me the stirring spoon.

"You first, just in case it's a bug," I said, when I realized we were sharing.

"They're raisins," she answered sharply.

"I meant a bug, like a virus."

"Oh."

We both looked in the pot, then at each other and giggled.

Lynn ate her typical smidgen of food and handed me the pot. She got up and began to break up camp. Her squirrel-like busyness seemed more agitated than usual, but then I wasn't myself either.

I ate a little oatmeal and gave Parker the rest. I stretched my legs, wiggled my toes, and rotated my ankles. There was a delay between the brain's request and the action. I could see but not feel all the movements.

Lynn had gathered our things into tidy piles near our backpacks, then returned to me. "Doing any better?"

"A little, maybe," I said, hoping it was true.

She shifted her eyes away as if considering my answer. I watched as she took the empty pot to the creek. She returned with it filled with water and set it back on the fire. When the water was warm enough, I cleaned the spoon and pot. Then, taking precarious steps, I moved to the backpacks braced against a pine tree and tucked the cookware in its appropriate place. Upon completing this simple task I sat down next to the packs.

I had been able to move, but was uncertain if it meant physical improvement or pure determination. My medically trained mind raced through symptoms and possible causes. The weighty compression in my chest barred deep breathing. It could be flu or soreness from excessive laughing. The throbbing deep in the hip sockets, along with my stiff back and shoulders, would not be unexpected after walking nine miles carrying a heavy load. As for the lack of feeling in my legs, had I pinched a nerve? I tried stretching again, first one leg and then the other, from the hip down. No matter how hard I tried, the exercise was futile. Were my brain functions also impaired? Did I blow a fuse last night?

Lynn emptied the tent and brought our clothes and miscellaneous gear to me, which I put in the packs. She took down the tent and brought it to me. I secured it on her pack while she checked her sleeping bag. The heat of the fire had done little to dry it and the pungent odor intensified. She stuffed the dry portion of her bag into the sack, and cleverly left the wet portion hanging out. I had just finished strapping on the tent when Lynn put her arm on my shoulder.

"Not doing so well, are you?"

My head dropped. A few tears dripped onto the carpet of dirt, grass, and pine needles.

"No I'm not," I mumbled. "I don't understand this."

Lynn crouched down beside me and took my face in her hands. She tenderly wiped the tear streaks, placed my head on her shoulder, and wrapped her arms around me.

"What can I do?" she asked.

"Exactly what you're doing." I shivered. Her embrace consumed me. I was warm and protected. I nestled closer. This was not a misreading. Lynn was not a touchy-feely person. I savored her tenderness and wished that it would never stop.

But she lessened her hold. "I think we need to turn back."

I jerked to attention. "No. We're more than half way. We made a plan. We have to finish what we started."

"We know what lies behind us," Lynn argued, "but neither of us has been beyond this point. It's safer to go back."

"It may be safer. But this isn't about safety," I said defiantly. "I can do this."

Lynn glanced at the well-worn path we had traveled. "Diana, be reasonable. We shouldn't even be debating this. I may not know what's wrong with you, but it's obvious you don't feel well. The sensible decision is to go back."

"It's not sensible. Over half the trail is already behind us. We're ahead of schedule, so we can take it slowly. Our husbands are expecting us up ahead." Lynn knew I had a point.

My head felt like it was veiled with fog, which made it hard for me to argue with her.

"The map indicates greater changes in elevation ahead, which means rougher terrain, and the trail is narrower," she said. "What if it's rocky and more steep?"

"Lynn. The adventure is this way," I said, waving my arm in the direction we hadn't yet traveled. I knew she'd cave to my authority, assuming I still had any.

"OK," she said in surrender. I gave an inner sigh of relief. She looked back one more time at the familiar path.

Lynn lifted my pack up for me. I braced myself for the weight, tightened the waistband, and took a tentative step. My legs worked. She placed her pack up on a rock, stooped down, and maneuvered into the shoulder straps. Standing up, she lifted the pack to her shoulders, fastened it, and the pack settled on her hips.

Parker and I were already on the move. I saw Lynn scan the camp. We were zealous about burning or carrying out our litter or any we found on our journeys. The site was clean. The fire was out. Lynn fell in behind us.

The trail definitely had more of a slope, both ascending and descending. Tree limbs and scrub oak branches brushed against my pack, threatening to push me off the path. I had to increase my effort to focus my mind and send messages to my legs. After several hundred yards I spied a group of rocks that looked just right to support our butts and packs. I walked off the trail to take advantage of the rest stop.

Lynn followed, bumping into me. "I'm sorry. I didn't know you were stopping."

"Great place for a little break," I said, panting.

"Do you need your pack off?"

"No, just a little rest."

I lay back against my pack and closed my eyes. I sensed Lynn checking me out, but I couldn't keep from falling asleep. I awoke with a start when Lynn moved.

"You OK?" she asked.

"I'll be OK."

I tucked my chin to my chest to stretch my knotted neck muscles, then used the boulder I was leaning against to leverage myself back to standing.

As the trail descended it narrowed and we had to scoot between an outcropping of thorny bushes. We emerged and came upon a field of pink and white boulders. They were the size and shape of Volkswagens, devoid of any signs of life. The creek we had been following disappeared somewhere in the sweeping expanse of giant rocks, then plunged into hidden realms.

There was no sign of a trail, just up and over each massive boulder. After a short distance Lynn started to scout out the easiest path through the obstacle course.

Parker made her way with an occasional boost and hardly a slip. Lynn helped me as I struggled to hold my own. This had been my call. I set my mind to command my body. I slid off the last boulder, stumbled forward, and lay sprawled out in the dirt.

"Are you OK?"

"Yeah."

My temples felt swollen from the extreme concentration. The feeling had never returned to my legs. All day, I had been lifting each leg's dead weight with my mind and willing it to safe placement. Where I had fallen was fine with me. I just needed to rest.

"Have you been watching the sky?" Lynn asked.

"The sky? My god, woman, no!" I exclaimed. "I had to scale rocks the size of bulldozers."

"Diana," she said urgently, "the clouds are piling up fast and the temperature is dropping. There's a storm coming. You must feel it."

I held up a hand to feel the air. It was cold and damp. I tucked it back under me in the dirt and drifted off to sleep.

I vaguely felt my shoulders being rocked back and forth, which forced my face deeper into the dirt. There was a tug on my arms and a weight pulled off my back. Lynn's voice woke me.

"Diana, you've got to wake up!"

I felt a hand around my arm. With her help I rolled over and looked up. Dark clouds covered half the sky.

"Perhaps water or food will help," she said.

I nodded. She handed me a canteen and I took a drink. I gagged when the water hit my parched mouth. I took another sip and the water soothed my throat. Parker was lying quietly at my side.

I heard Lynn say loudly, "Diana, the storm . . ." Then her voice faded and I fell asleep again.

"Diana, you can't sleep anymore."

"What?" I asked, annoyed. Was I dreaming?

I forced myself back to consciousness. "How long have I been asleep?"

"An hour." Lynn's voice was shrill as she pointed at the sky. I looked upward at the dark gray-green sky. Lynn typically panicked in adverse situations and it was up to me to calm her and get her refocused.

I knew I needed to pull myself together, but my mental faculties were like a windshield wiper on a slow speed. I barely got a clear view when things blurred again. The nap had failed to revitalize me. I tried hard to focus. This was not Lynn overreacting. This was serious. There was no existing shelter and nowhere to put a tent. I'd fallen on the only patch of soft dirt.

"What time is it?" I asked.

"Two."

It seemed later. The clouds had moved in very fast and the temperature had definitely dropped.

"While you slept I found a place," Lynn said, "just a little farther where we could set up a camp. I know you're tired, but you've got to try." She lifted my pack onto my shoulders. "Is that OK?"

I glanced up at the ominous sky. "So far, so good."

Lynn nodded and attended to her own pack. Parker was panting at my feet. Lynn offered her arm for support. I took it. Pride and ego were gone. Gone also was the ability to do more than one thing at a time. Right now I focused solely on following Lynn.

I was oblivious to distance. If there was a slope or a rock, did I place my foot on the rock or alongside of it? If I judged just right the swing of my hip would make my foot land squarely. If I was wrong I could twist my ankle, stumble, or go down. All I could deal with was one foot in front of the other, one step at a time. I wanted to close my eyes to ease the strain of such intense concentration. Though I felt no bruising or pain in my legs, the jolt of each fall resonated through my upper body and neck, which intensified my headache. Lynn would help me back up. We'd go on. It's what we had to do.

"It's not much farther," she encouraged after yet another fall. She grabbed my shaking hand and pulled me up once again.

"We'll leave your pack. I'll come and get it later. We must get to where I can pitch a tent. We're definitely going to need the shelter tonight." She removed my pack. A tear lingered near her chin.

"I don't know what's come over me." I wiped the tear from her chin. "I'm sorry. I utterly despise being a burden."

Lynn had to support me to get my legs to hold me, even without the pack. We were both freezing cold.

"Where's that coming from?" I asked.

"What?"

"The music."

"What music?"

"The rock-and-roll music."

Lynn pierced me with her eyes. "There is no music, Diana."

"It's so loud and annoying, surely you can hear it," I said, in disbelief. "Come and listen, it's in my right ear."

Dutifully she put her ear to mine. "I don't hear anything."

We walked on, soaked from the damp air, Lynn in silence and me hearing a very annoying beat.

I collapsed at the new campsite. Lynn fluffed my sleeping bag out and spread it over me. Over that she put a tarp.

When I opened my eyes there was a cup of hot chocolate beside me, a blazing fire, and the tent was up.

"Supper's ready," Lynn said. "Can you stay awake long enough to eat?"

"I feel drugged."

Lynn grasped my hand and lifted me up. My legs wobbled like jello and were numb. The aches I could feel from my crawl across the boulders and the falls on the hard trail, were all above the waist. Lynn picked up the cup of hot chocolate, placed my arm over her shoulder, and walked me to a place by the fire.

The fire was warm. I accepted the packet of hot lasagna and ate to appease Lynn.

"Lynn, I am so sorry. I've ruined everything."

"I'm really worried. Tell me what's going on with you."

I put the food and spoon down. "I don't know. It's not like any flu I've ever known."

"You're hearing things that aren't there." Lynn's voice started to rise. "This is no flu."

I cringed, covered my ears, and began to cry, which quickly grew into body-wracking sobs. Outraged at my weakness, I slammed my fists into my thighs and pain shot from my shoulders down my back. I wrapped my arms around my chest. The pain and frustration made my head pound.

"I've never felt like this and I just can't shake it," I cried out.

Lynn was behind me, easing me back to rest against her body. She worked her hands between my hat and coat collar to find my neck. Her gentle rubbing brought warmth to my muscles. I began to relax. Parker lay over my feet.

"Do you still hear music?" Lynn asked in a soothing tone.

"Music?" I had forgotten that. "No, why, do you want to dance?" I giggled. "I can hardly walk, but I would love to dance with you."

Lynn stopped rubbing, then quietly chuckled.

I sat as long as I could, taking pleasure in Lynn's touch. "I'm sorry. I've got to lie down."

"Your sleeping bag is ready."

I just wanted to crawl right in, but Lynn insisted I change from my damp clothes. She helped with each article of clothing. This could have been fun. I was beyond fun. When I was ready for bed, she unzipped my bag, and flung it open. I rolled in and instantly fell asleep.

I heard Lynn saying, "Diana, I'm freezing. It's so c-c-cold. My bag is still wet, do you think I could get in yours?" I opened my eyes and saw Lynn's face hovering above me.

"Of course," I replied. The material of her sleeping bag made crinkling noises as she climbed out. It had been light when I went to bed, but it was dark now.

"How long have I been asleep?" I asked as Lynn squirmed in beside me.

"A couple of hours."

I felt the arctic invasion. Lynn trembled violently. "You're freezing. You should have climbed in earlier." I worked my arms and legs around her, then began to rub her body to warm her more quickly. She responded by cuddling in, better than a puppy, which reminded me. "Parker, where's Parker?"

"In my bag," Lynn shuddered.

There were damp places along her back. "You're wet!"

"Condensation. I must have brushed against the tent walls."

"Are you warming up?"

"Yes, thank you. I hated to wake you. I just couldn't get warm. How are you feeling?"

"Besides useless?"

"You're not useless. You're warming me up."

Lynn put her arm around me, massaging along my spine. With each squeeze, I willed the muscles to release so she could press deeper and deeper. I slipped my hands under her thermal nightwear rubbing gently. I could feel her shivering diminish as she became warmer. A faint scent of apple wafted from her soft skin. I pressed closer.

She wiggled and our embrace tightened. "Thank you, Diana. I didn't think I'd ever get warm." Those were the last words I heard before I sank into a deep sleep.

# CHAPTER FIVE

TIGHTLY ENTWINED, WE had slept through the night. The intimacy made me smile with pleasure. Somehow Lynn had inched out without waking me. My bag was dry, warm, and comfortable. The music was off, my headache was moderate, and I could think about our situation. While the music thumped loudly in my head, it was nearly impossible to think. As I saw it, we had each other, our supplies, shelter, and all-weather sleeping bags. We should stay, make the best of the situation and wait. When we don't show up to meet our husbands today, surely they'll send a rescue party.

The tent flap opened and in the gray light Lynn's smiling face appeared. "Would you like Sunday breakfast in bed?"

I smiled back. "Yes, that would be lovely."

Lynn came back with a pot of oatmeal and two cups of coffee. I sipped the coffee and took a couple of bites from the pot, then gave it to Lynn.

"That's for you," she said and pushed the pot back toward me. "I'm fine with coffee for now."

"You've got to eat to keep your strength up," I insisted.

"You go ahead. When I get nervous I can't eat. There's snow 50 feet up the hill from our tent. Diana, I need to know the truth. How are you this morning? We're in a serious situation."

I was surprised at Lynn's tone. She must be scared. Typically Lynn gave me information and I told her what to do.

"Lynn, it'll be all right." I took her hand. "We can stay right here."

"No, Diana, we can't stay here!"

I winced and my headache intensified.

She noticed and reduced her volume. "The storm isn't breaking up. We could get dumped on. Diana, you're not well, not at all yourself. I think we need to get the heck out of here to make it to our lunch rendezvous. Are you going to be able to carry a pack?"

This was happening too fast. My processing skills were too slow. Why did she insist we keep moving?

"We can skip the lunch meet and just stay here."

"The lunch meet is why we continued this way instead of turning back. Remember your goal, stick to the plan?"

"Well, it doesn't seem as important now."

"It's more important than ever."

Lynn had exercised great control and patience all this time, but now I watched befuddled as she stashed some of our supplies behind a bush and packed the rest of the camp. She dismantled the tent and strapped it to her pack. With my pack in tow she stood ready to slip it over my shoulders. My knees buckled. Instantly, Lynn lifted up the pack. I locked my stance and my knees held the weight. I was not going to fall anymore. We were both covered in bruises.

Lynn stayed next to me whenever the trail allowed. The sky was a dome of heavy clouds. The path narrowed as it wove along the edge of the shallow stream. Periodically we were forced to walk in the water. The uneven creek bed and murmuring water acted like a tranquilizer and made it increasingly difficult to focus. I had to keep my legs taut, almost locking my knees to stay upright. Parker ran and splashed her way through the creek. Her exuberance helped to keep me on the move.

Suddenly Lynn stopped. I shot a look at her. She turned pale as her eyes swept the area.

"What?" I asked.

"The trail, where is it?" she wailed.

I looked; two more steps and it was all water. The only trail I saw was the one we had just come down. A beaver had dammed the creek's flow, causing the stream to inch over its natural boundaries to form a pond.

I was tired. The throbbing beat had returned. "What does it matter? This is a good place to rest."

Lynn helped me remove my pack and then took off her own. "This beat in my head makes me dizzy."

"Perhaps it's a fever doing this to you." Touching my forehead, she compared the temperature to that of my cheeks, then shook her head. "No fever. I'll see about a way around this pond. This wasn't on our trail map. Will you be all right?"

"Sure." This was a perfect excuse for a rest. I braced my back against a rock, slid onto the ground, and peered into the pool, searching in the water for fish, frogs, or turtles.

*On the water Ben and Paula appeared merrily dancing through ribbons that were fluttering downward from the sky. Their youthful laughs faded as a cloud of smoke pushed in and my mother's ashen face took shape. Her hair was meticulously styled, and though her lips were moving, there was no sound. I tried to speak to her, but I had no voice.*

I stirred. Where was Mom and why couldn't we communicate? I searched the pond. She was gone, as were my children who had looked so carefree and happy just moments ago.

It took a moment after the dream ended to get my bearings. Where was Lynn? I had been hiking with Lynn. I tried to call for her, but I couldn't hear my voice over the pulsing beat in my head. I tried again but my voice was even weaker.

Desperately I started rummaging through our packs for the map or a compass. I ransacked the plastic-wrapped bundles of clothing and foil packets of food. I pulled out the pot and utensils. I was exhausted and lay my head down to rest.

Lynn's voice woke me. "Whatever were you doing?"

Parker was happily sniffing the contents of the backpack, which were strewn all around me.

"I didn't know where you were. I had to find you."

"In your backpack?" Lynn asked.

"No. I had to get the map."

The music had stopped. My face and hands were cold. Had I hallucinated about my children and my mother?

Lynn shook her head as she picked up two energy bars from off the ground, handed one to me, and unwrapped the other for herself. She took a bite. "Here's the situation." Suddenly she pinched her lips together, her throat muscles contracting. She turned and ran to the bushes where she vomited. She wiped her mouth with a tissue. "I'm so sorry, that was disgusting. I know better than to eat when I'm upset." She passed me what was left of her energy bar.

"You've got to be kidding." I tucked both bars into my coat pocket. "I can't eat this now."

Ice crystals sifted through the air.

"I skirted a long way around the pond," Lynn said, quickly. "It's marshy, sometimes deep, and very slick in places. I didn't find the trail. Dian a, somehow we took a wrong turn. We have to go back."

"Go back? Let's just stay here. There's water. We can make a nice camp."

"Have you noticed that it's snowing and we're going to get dumped on? We're in a canyon down here and it could fill with snow. We need to get out of here now!"

"I wish you would relax a little. This peaceful setting is a perfect place to camp, get warm, stay dry, and rest."

"Relax!" Lynn said. "Damn it, Diana. With all this tree cover we'll never be found down here."

That seemed fine to me, quite wonderful really. Lynn, Parker. and I, warm and toasty in a tent covered with snow. It would be so quiet, unless that horrible music came back.

"Diana, you're scaring me. You need medical attention. We've got to get out of here." Lynn stuffed things into the pack.

She was scared, hyped-up, and acting impulsively. She wasn't thinking big picture. That was my job and I was off duty.

I said nothing as she hoisted the pack onto my back, secured it, and literally pushed me into motion. Going uphill was a real struggle. I had to mentally gauge and guide each step. Even so I tripped a few times, fell, and dragged myself through portions of the trail. When we eventually made it back to our last camp, I instantly plopped down, using a tree for support.

Lynn offered me water. I drank.

"You have to drink, too."

"I can't. It just comes back up."

Now lucid, the headache a dull pain, I said, "Then you're dehydrated. You have to drink a little at a time."

Lynn took just enough to moisten her mouth. "Why don't you eat that bar now?"

"I just need to rest a bit. Then I'll help you with camp."

"Camp? We're not staying here. We must get back."

"Back where? Why?"

"We're both sick."

Yes, we were both sick now. Lynn's heaving had made that abundantly clear. I had to be mindful of that. "You should drink more water."

"The storm is here," she said, taking a very small sip. "Search planes can't fly in bad storms. Snowmobiles can't travel these trails without snowpack. Horses can't walk through a mass of boulders." It took all I had to hear what she said. My mind was mush.

"And you think we can?" I was beyond having any confidence in myself. Was Lynn right? She had certainly considered the rescue options. Could I rely on my judgment? I saw and heard things that weren't there!

"We'll leave your gear here with a note in case it's found." She placed items she'd hidden at this camp earlier, along with our dirty clothes, out in the open to attract attention. She gathered rocks and formed an arrow to indicate the direction in which we were headed. The map, food, cooking gear, matches, a flashlight, and some clean clothes were stuffed into her pack. The tent and sleeping bag were strapped to the outside. I followed Lynn, trusting she knew where to go.

With my focus on the immediate trail, I was stunned when I looked up and saw the field of boulders again. Parker had been happily leading the way with her puppy inquisitiveness. Now she sat next to me, looking directly into the base of the stone wall in front of us, the first of many.

When I stood still, Lynn said, "We have to keep moving."

Together we slowly worked our way over and through the stone fortress. Back and forth she went, first with the pack and then with me.

"Wake up, Diana, you're almost there. Last climb, let's go."

I was groggy and just wanted to sleep, but Lynn pulled me along. It seemed so far, so many steps, so much climbing. It was inevitable, with no feeling in my legs and no visual of what was below me, that I would fall, shredding clothes and skin.

"Diana!"

I had no breath to respond. I tried to draw air. Sharp pains radiated through my chest. I felt snowflakes melt on my face. Then Lynn was there. "Lie still. What hurts?"

"What doesn't?" I whispered.

She pushed Parker away before the pup could leap onto my chest. "Not now, Parker. I know it hurts, but are you OK?"

"Hell, no!" I responded. How could she even ask that?

She flinched.

"I'm sorry. I'm not OK. You're not OK. And this whole damn mess is fucking not OK!" I said this through unchecked tears.

She felt my legs. "Can you feel this?"

"Haven't in days," I said.

There was a noticeable pause. I looked and found her face white. Hadn't I told her?

"Days?"

"Hours? Days? I don't know. All kinds of crazy going on in here," I said, grabbing my head.

"I saw that you had trouble moving your legs, but I didn't know you couldn't feel them."

"No, I can't, not at all."

"Diana, didn't you think you should tell me?"

"I didn't want you to worry."

"Not worry? Are you kidding me? I've been terrified watching you stumble and fall. And sometimes what you're saying doesn't make any sense. I don't know what's happening to you, but we must get you to safety." Lynn paused, then gathered herself. "You have to help me get you over this last boulder. Can you try?"

"I can't." Crying had lessened the stuffy feeling in my head, but I was physically drained.

"You must." She stood over me, offering her hand.

"I'm done. You go. Take Parker."

"Parker? I don't need a dog. I need you."

Her sweet words made me want to take her hand. Despite Lynn's attempt to ease me down the last boulder, I fell in a heap. Parker nuzzled me as Lynn rolled me on my back to assess my condition before she scanned the landscape. She helped me up and led me to a seat on the low branch of a pine tree. I leaned against the trunk and let my mind roam freely, distorting past events into a kaleidoscope of visions.

*LOOKING DOWN THE barrel of a gun, I sat frozen on a couch with perspiration beading up and dripping from my face. My tension eased as beautiful colored sparks burst into a fireworks display shooting from the gun barrel. But my eye burned from the flaring ember. I scurried away from the hay; any tiny cinder would set it ablaze and all would see. The secret would be out. He would hit my brother. I ran, and ran and ran, but they caught me.*

*My stepfather led the board members on to shout, "Stupid little girl with stupid ideas." They grabbed and shook me. But I wouldn't be shaken so I made myself rigid, and I fell to the ground where I stayed unyielding. I was tired of giving in to them. I wouldn't give in now.*

IT WAS A relief to wake to the sound of Lynn calling my name and tugging on my arm. She half carried me back to our first campsite and helped me down near the base of a tall, leafless tree. Parker was wagging her tail and sniffing the grasses, undaunted by the fading sun and frigid temperature.

Lynn shuffled about with a slight limp as she erected our tent, put the damp pack inside to protect it from additional exposure, and spread the sleeping bag out. She pulled out the backpacker's stove and started to heat water. I don't know how I got into the tent, but Lynn began stripping off my damp, torn, and blood-encrusted clothes.

"I'm sorry," Lynn said. "This must really hurt. Your jeans are stuck to you but they've got to come off."

I could barely make out her words with the music constantly drumming in my head. "It's OK. It doesn't hurt. I can't feel it."

"These wounds should be cleaned but it's too cold, and I just can't." Lynn helped me pull on my dry pajamas.

Her face was drawn tight, her body had a tremor much like a plucked guitar string.

"Lynn, you're exhausted. I'm so sorry. You need to rest too."

She nodded and joined me in the sleeping bag. We snuggled so tightly together that our two worn out bodies became warm, and we quickly fell asleep.

In the morning Lynn unfastened the zipper and popped out like a kernel of exploding popcorn. She hit her head on the sagging tent, drops of water fell on her hair and beads of condensation rolled down the walls. Then we heard a scraping sound and a mass slid down the outside wall. She hurriedly unzipped a few inches of the tent fly. Parker anxiously pushed out for her morning duties.

Lynn took a peek. "It snowed." Her words were as crisp as the mountain air. "Everything is covered!" She pulled the zipper back down. "It's freezing. Our clothes are damp."

I smiled.

"How can you be so calm?" she snapped, rubbing her hands together.

"It's magical here. I'm warm. I'm lying down. There's no boulder field, board meeting, company crisis, or raving husband to deal with."

"You've lost it, Diana. We need help, not jokes."

I could see her shivering. I opened the sleeping bag and she climbed in, absorbing the warmth that radiated from me. She burrowed close. I slept.

Lynn was already up when I woke. She helped me dress and get out to pee. The campfire she'd made had melted the ankle-deep snow nearly a foot out from the firepit. The sky was brighter now and the air not as dense.

"They could be searching for us today since we didn't meet Dick and William yesterday, but we can't count on it," Lynn said. "I thought there would be other people camped here last night, but there aren't. We have to get back to the jeep."

I shook my head. "If you're going, you're going without me. For all I know it may be the moving around that's making my condition worse. We're both exhausted and sick, you're dehydrated and I just want to sleep. The camp is set up. To take it down and set it back up is a waste of energy."

Was dehydration affecting her decision making as my illness did mine? She had left my bag, my pack, and other equipment, thinking there would be help here.

"Yesterday almost killed us. It's insane to think we can handle nine miles through snow today." I hoped that I had spoken rationally, but the effort had taken its toll. "I've got to lie down now."

"I'll clear a place outside so you can feel the sun." Lynn paused briefly, looked to the sky, and then walked to the only rock in the center of our small clearing. She dusted it off with her boot and brushed the snow from a small flat area next to it. She opened a tightly-folded, space-age foil blanket and spread it over the dirt. My resting place readied, she came for me. She helped me sit down and carefully wrapped the excess foil around my battered body. I pulled it over my face and drifted off.

# CHAPTER SIX

"DIANA! DIANA! WAKE up!" Her words were a faint irritant from the depth of my sleep. She charged past me and I opened my eyes in surprise. She was searching the snow-filled sky.

I glanced up and saw nothing. A false alarm. Having moved only my eyes, settling back was easy. The music had stopped, but the thunderous sound of a stampede took its place.

That woke me. I looked in the direction where Lynn stood. *Apocalypse Now*, I thought. It was like the movie but there was just one helicopter with blades whirling, lifting over the treetops.

Lynn shouted as she ran, her arms fluttering through the air like a hummingbird. Her presence could hardly go unnoticed. The helicopter slowly passed, turned, came back, and hovered above our campsite. The air swirled with snow. My face was bombarded and the foil blanket flapped. Parker squeezed her body underneath mine.

The wind and noise intensified as the helicopter circled lower, weaving first to one side and then the other. Snowflakes and sparks rose and collided in the whirlwind to create a spectacular shimmering vortex. The trees leaned away from the force of the wind made by the blades. Everything was being whipped and swirled, including the cacophony of sound in my head.

I hoisted myself up as best I could, leaning on the pack. Lynn ran to me, and I threw my arm around her neck. She struggled to stand while holding me up. The storm increased in its ferocity, as the wind and snow battered the helicopter. It rocked back and forth as it tried to land. Then Lynn and I stood in shocked disbelief as we watched the helicopter leave. The noise slowly diminished. The quiet was stark.

Then as if she had been hit by a jolt of electricity, Lynn jumped into action. She dismantled our camp and made numerous trips with our gear to cache it on the trail, where she anticipated a Search and Rescue team would arrive. I watched as she and Parker scurried about like two squirrels prepping for winter, then I fell asleep.

I awoke at Lynn's voice. "Thank God you found us," she said repeatedly. "I couldn't leave her. She fell asleep every time we stopped moving and she woke up in a stupor."

Suddenly next to me I heard a calm, deep voice. "What's wrong, honey?"

"She can't walk," Lynn answered.

"Ma'am?" the man said.

"Yes?" I said weakly.

"Describe to me what's wrong."

"My legs don't move. They just won't work."

"Did that happen as the result of a fall?" he asked as he swept his eyes over my body.

"It was before she fell," Lynn said.

"No," I said. "I just woke up and they were numb."

"Any other problems?"

The list was long. I narrowed it to, "I heard loud rock-and-roll music in my right ear and my chest felt compressed, like when my lungs collapsed, but that's gone now."

"But you've been traveling like this for how long?"

"Two or three days. I'm not sure."

"Since Saturday morning," Lynn said.

"And when did she fall?"

"Yesterday, coming back through a field of boulders after the trail vanished into a beaver pond." Lynn glanced behind us.

"Excuse us, please. Stretcher coming through."

Two other men from the rescue team approached.

"She's been impaired since Saturday," my rescuer told them. "I doubt there could be any harm in moving her now." To me he said, "They're going to put you on the stretcher. Just let them lift you."

Their hands moved around and under my neck, shoulders, butt, and legs. Up and over I went. After I was secured in place they lifted the stretcher and started on the trail.

I awoke as I was being passed through the hatch of an all-terrain vehicle. More straps were fastened and the door was closed. I could feel the bumps of the road as the ATV crunched through the snow.

I heard a man ask Lynn, "Would you remove your jacket so I can get your blood pressure?" I slept.

The arctic air woke me as the door opened and bright white snowflakes falling from heaven made me blink. The men moved me out of the vehicle and toward the ambulance, with Lynn alongside. Dick appeared, spun her toward him and held her in an embrace. He was stopped by Parker who popped her head out of the jacket just beneath Lynn's chin and growled.

"What?" Dick yelped.

"She's fine—a little dehydrated but fine," one of the rescuers told Dick. "She's OK to go home. Liquids often and in very small amounts."

"Thank goodness! Oh, thank God."

The rescue workers placed my stretcher in the snow and huddled around me, their fingers feeling their way under me from head to foot.

"On three. One. Two. Three."

Up I went, just inches off the ground. I could hear the stretcher being pulled out from under me.

"Coming under." Then a second stretcher slid beneath me.

"Ready? Lower on three. One. Two. Three."

I could see Lynn watch as the straps and blanket were adjusted and I was lifted into the ambulance. Then I heard William speaking to the rescue team.

"I made the call to get you here. She's my wife. What is her condition? Tell me. I'm not some twit I'm a doctor."

Turning toward the sounds, I saw William's head bob over Lynn and the ambulance crew. He was there. Of course he would be: in his way he did care about me. He ducked in quickly, before they could close the door. "Diana, say something, honey." He was pulled back before I could answer. The door closed.

"I want to be with my wife."

"You can meet us at Park View Hospital."

A loud tap on the window startled me. William waved and yelled, "I'll see you at the hospital, love."

The ambulance pulled away. I was glad for the quiet. I thought of how Lynn stayed at my side until the ambulance door closed. Then my private concert began in my right ear.

Sirens and lights seemed to penetrate my skull when the rear door of the ambulance opened. I was loaded on a gurney and wheeled into the emergency room where doctors came from several directions and bombarded me with questions. The clamor of noise and blaze of lights made me want to go back to sleep.

# CHAPTER SEVEN

MY FILTHY BODY and battle-frayed camp clothes were brilliantly illuminated under the glare of the hospital lights. Occasionally I'd get a whiff of the sanitized air over the smell of smoke that had permeated my pores and clothes. We hadn't bathed or used deodorant since the morning we left. I couldn't fathom how long that had been. I tried to recount the days of our adventure. I smiled at the thought of Lynn's body snug against mine. One hospital attendant untied my scuffed leather boots while another used a gleaming pair of scissors to cut the mangled trousers free from my body.

"Get an EKG, stat," a doctor ordered.

Glancing around the room, I saw Lynn just outside the doorway.

"What is wrong with her? What can I do?" Lynn asked.

William was there, his eyebrows raised and his lips tightly pressed together in a downward curve.

A nurse led him away by the arm. "Let's get the paperwork completed. Do you have insurance? We'll need a copy of the card."

I became aware of a nurse cutting off my sweatshirt. The staff, a medical version of crime scene investigators, seemed intent on collecting specimens and studying the evidence. I chuckled silently at being an unsolved mystery. Sherlock Holmes would have said, "The game is afoot."

"We need blood work, stat. Have the lab run a full panel."

"Diana," a male voice asked. "Can you feel me touching the bottom of your foot?"

"No," I whispered.

"Do you feel anything now? Diana, you've got to stay with me. Open your eyes," he demanded, briskly shaking me. His narrow sharp-featured face was framed by the darkness of my drooping eyelids. But more importantly, at the outer periphery of the privacy curtain I saw Paula, wide-eyed with tears rolling down her cheeks. Our eye contact was blocked instantly by a shadowy figure of a woman saying, "Please. All of you must go to the waiting room. We need to do our workup."

"But . . ." Paula said in protest. She was a force, not easily moved.

"We'll let you know as soon as we know anything." The female shadow herded everyone out of the way.

Paula's and my devotion to one another was an intrinsic bond. It was another reason for me to be an example of a positive force in the world. My incapacitated body must not unravel her belief in Mom the Unstoppable. I needed to console her and assure her I would be fine. She shouldn't stress out over me. It wasn't good for her or the baby, but I'd been too slow; she was gone.

"Diana! Your toes," the doctor said, placing his face directly into my vision. "Can you move your toes?"

I sent the message to my toes. "Did they move?"

"Yes."

I felt the fog creeping over me again and I succumbed to its heavy blanket.

*CRAWLING AMIDST THE aromatic, soft, freshly cut hay, I snuggled, getting smaller as I went deeper and deeper so as to be unseen. If I lay very still perhaps I would be hidden. But this was not a safe place. I could not hide in the hayloft.*

*Hearing his boots firm on the steps as he ascended the rickety homemade ladder, gave me a warning, but there was no escape. To run, I'd learned, was useless. I very quietly took a shallow breath. Any slight movement or sound would be detected. There was a faint brushing noise from hay falling through the rungs of the ladder. He shuffled in my direction. There was a deep gurgling to his laugh as he rifled the loose hay I had over me.*

*His smelly breath and bristly face were the least of his assault as he fell upon me.*

WHEN I OPENED my eyes there was no fog. There were, instead, white walls, the smell of rubbing alcohol and bleeping devices. The thin blanket covering me was twisted from my thrashing. I was sweaty, cold, and sore. The bass notes of my private band reverberated in my ears. I looked around the dim room. Small red and green lights blinked.

I recalled an ambulance, bright lights, doctors, and questions—endless questions. But now I was alone, totally alone. I had been in the hospital enough times to know how to get answers. I made snow angels on the bed to find the nurse callbox. I pushed the button. Within seconds a male nurse appeared at my bedside.

"Can I help you?" he asked in a calm voice.

"Yes," I said quickly so as not to lose my thoughts and drift once again into another realm. "What time is it? What is wrong with me? Where are my daughter and my friends?"

"My dear, it's 5:30 a.m. No visitors now. We don't know what's wrong yet. We've run tests, we're tracking your heart rhythm and waiting for lab results. The doctor will be in later. Is there anything you need?"

"No." Then I added, "Another blanket, please."

"Certainly," the nurse said. The crinkling of his crisp white uniform drew my attention to the elongated stride of his beanpole legs as he left the room.

*THE ENGULFING WHITE became low clouds and snow whorls. Lynn leapt naked in pirouettes through the luminescent crystals like a prima ballerina. She moved with amorphous entities that served only to enhance her performance. The gold, blue, red, and white spotlights added dazzling highlights to the contours of her muscled body as she danced against*

*backgrounds of windmills, rainbows, and grand ballrooms.
Then she beckoned me. I tried to enter into the scene for a dance
with her. But the curtain fell.*


MY RECENT EVENTS, past history, and dreams had
woven together like an ethereal tapestry. There was no sense
of time in the intensive care unit. The sun had no impact on
the cycles of day and night in the room. When I was moved
to a different room I sensed Paula was with me. I never felt
William's presence.

*The sun's rays shot past the person who stood in the doorway.
She faced away from me, odd in her statue-like pose. "Do
you want something?" I asked. The woman turned, revealing
her long nose with black-rimmed glasses resting thereon. My
mother's tender message, "Diana, I want to help you," delivered
with a hard cold glare confused me.*

I wanted more from my mother. How did she help me? Did
she know what was happening? Could she overcome Dad's
domination? After all this time, pointless as it was, I still longed
for her help. But Mother was gone.

"Paula, you know how to reach me."

At the sound of a woman's voice saying my daughter's name,
I opened my eyes. Paula was sitting beside the bed.

"I will, Kathleen," Paula said. "Thank you."

"You're here?" I said.

Paula stood and leaned over me. "Of course, Mom. Kathleen
and Steve are here, too."

I looked around to see my computer tech genius, Steve,
and his wife, Kathleen, in the shadows on the other side of
the bed.

Steve took my hand in his bear-size paw. "Diana, you must
not worry about the company. You need to save your strength
and come back to us." He stepped back and his tall, hefty frame
was replaced by his wife's lithesome figure.

She took my hand in her cool grasp. "We are here for you."

I started to cry. "I trust you to watch over our dream."

"I'll keep an eagle eye on everything and everyone," Steve said, with tears forming.

I smiled, knowing that this gentle giant, who sat at his computer all day, would indeed have an eagle eye on the specialized operations and blustery egos that managed Pioneering. Steve was the first person I recruited to help me get the company started. His wife, Kathleen, a stay-at-home mother of two, would host our never-ending meetings and serve delicious meals as we strategized the birth of Pioneering. Her stability was the perfect balance to his high-tech mind.

"We're so glad the rescue team found you before the storm got worse," Kathleen said.

"Found?" I said.

"William said you were lost," Paula said.

"But I was never lost," I said, agitated.

Then my body convulsed and Paula urgently shouted for a nurse. I caught the look of fear on Kathleen's face before I was engulfed in writhing agony.

I woke later to Lynn's warm hand closed gently around mine. My heart leapt.

"Diana, what have they told you?" she whispered urgently. "You've got to tell me. What can I do?"

Had they told me something? Why couldn't I remember?

Paula stepped into the room. "Lynn, I don't think Mom knows much of anything."

My hand dropped from Lynn's grasp to the cool sheets.

"Perhaps tomorrow. We should let her sleep." Paula stood between Lynn and me. Paula escorted Lynn to the door. "Shouldn't you be at home?"

I didn't want her to leave. "Lynn!"

"I'll be back," she called out to me.

Several voices sounded from the corridor, "Sh-h-h-h-h-h. This is a hospital."

"Thanks for being here," I whispered.

Paula returned and carefully put her arms through the various sensors I wore tracking my body functions to give me a hug. Her protective embrace made me sob uncontrollably.

"I've tried to keep everyone away," she said, then straightened and wiped away her own tears. She grabbed the tissue box, took one for herself, and handed it to me.

"It's OK," I said. "I've been so out of it. I think I'm better now. I just needed a day to sleep."

"A day? Are you kidding? It's been four days."

"Four days? I don't have time to lie around here."

"The doctor hasn't talked with you?" Paula asked.

"I . . . I . . . I don't know," I stammered. My stomach tightened. "What did he tell you?"

"It's still uncertain," Paula said, shaking her head.

"What's uncertain?" I inquired.

"Everything! They still don't know what happened to you."

I sensed her reluctance to tell me. "I know you're trying to protect me, but I need to know." I clenched my fists and gritted my teeth as I imagined what pinched nerve, virus, or other malady had befallen me.

"Mom, you'd best prepare yourself. William is right behind me. He just stopped at the water faucet to wipe up the coffee he spilled."

His presence, though unwelcome, was not nearly as bad as whatever secret diagnosis was lurking about that my daughter was unable to voice.

She gave me another careful hug. "I'd stay longer, but it's better if I'm not here with him. I'll be back in the morning." And with that she was gone.

I was a prisoner to all who came. The wires and tubes were a kind of bondage. Needles were adhered with skin-pinching tape and electrodes were glued to me, tracking my body's information. I was helpless and unable to escape.

I closed my eyes and lay very still to discourage William. He sauntered in, grabbed the clipboard from the foot of my bed, and hoisted himself up next to me on the mattress. He glanced over the clinical observations.

"You should look at this," he said, poking me as he displayed the near illegible penmanship.

Together we attempted to decode the notes. Grasping at the chance to know more, I deciphered the scrawl even though we sat closer than I wanted. We read, *"Inability to walk, profound memory lapses, lab tests negative, recommend that a neurologist see this patient. MRI revealed abnormal signals in the deep white matter tracks of the corona radialis at both right and left."*

"So the MRI was abnormal," I said.

"Brain lesions," William said. "Blimey good explanation for your behavior of late, love."

"William, that's not funny."

"No such intent. It's a perfectly logical explanation for why you've been acting so crazy lately."

"Get serious," I said. "Brain lesions? What caused them?"

I felt such white-hot rage that I thought I would explode. I lashed out against the horror, knocking the clipboard against William's chest. He slid from the bed, dropping the clipboard to catch himself. He ran his fingers through his hair, cocked his head slightly, sighed heavily, and looked at me.

"Please leave," I said, through gritted teeth. If I opened my mouth my words would sear him, and I didn't need to torch the messenger. I needed time to digest what no one had been willing to tell me, except William.

# CHAPTER EIGHT

TIME WAS MUDDLED for me but I was aware that it was slipping away while the hospital searched for a diagnosis. On occasion I labored to put a recognizable signature on paperwork from the office. It was a struggle to track each document, know what it meant, and be sure it was accurate. My reliance on Paula and Lynn grew. I had to get back to the office. I feared that the clash of other people's agendas would affect the company and ruin everything I had worked so hard for.

My analytical mind worked overtime trying to find a reason for what was happening to me. The relentless analyzing intensified my headaches. Delusions continued to haunt me. To sleep was as much about relief from pain and worry as it was about exhaustion. The rock and roll never played in my dreams.

William was with me for a very brief visit from a doctor.

"So much for bedside manner," William exclaimed. "What a bloody bastard. Let me go talk with him a bit further." He charged after the doctor.

I doubted he would have much success. His English charm worked better with women. Though intelligent and well-credentialed, William's air of self-importance often gave way to obnoxious superiority.

Minutes passed; the quiet was welcome. I reflected on my dependence on others in the past, which had almost always resulted in disappointment. My experience was that a show of vulnerability was an invitation to attack. Now I was fighting for my life; and the result was out of my hands.

William returned to the room. "Well, I know what is going on. Your assigned neurologist is a Dr. Waterford who gets $260 an hour and is supposedly one of the best." Hourly fee, yearly salary, or overall assets were William's means of determining a person's social clout and worthiness. "He'll be in sometime today."

"I hope I'm awake," I said.

William stared at me, his mouth working like a fish released from the hook and still gasping for breath on the riverbank. I surrendered to sleep.

A nurse shook me gently. "Diana, Dr. Waterford is here."

Struggling to climb out of the depths of sleep, I slowly opened my eyes to see a tall sliver of a man whose face was etched by 60 or so years of tending to the sick. His voice was deep as he directed the nurse to bring him a safety pin.

After a few minutes he finished his testing and told the nurse, "Bring me her records." He started toward the door.

"Stop!" Lynn burst out and I was suddenly aware of her and Paula's presence. "You can't leave us like this!"

"Pardon me?" He looked at Lynn and Paula, taking several moments to appraise them. "And you are?"

I was highly interested in how Lynn would explain her presence and our relationship.

"I . . . I . . ." Lynn stuttered, glancing at me.

"This is Lynn," Paula interjected. "She works for my Mom. I'm Paula, her daughter. We've been waiting for a diagnosis for so long and I was told that you could tell us more after your examination."

"I apologize. In summary, the X-rays confirm no broken ribs and no damage from your previous lung surgeries. We originally thought you had a heart condition, but that has been ruled out. Your heart is in good shape. However, you do have lesions on your brain, and we are attempting to find the cause."

Paula took my hand in hers. Lynn placed her hand on my shoulder.

The doctor watched and continued without pausing. "All the testing, including renal function, glucose metabolism, electrolytes, protein studies, lyme titer, liver function, HIV, lipid studies, and thyroid indicate you are healthy. Though the workups so far haven't substantiated any of them, your symptoms alone could suggest a number of diseases."

"Such as?" I questioned.

"You're a tough woman, Diana, to have hiked any distance in your condition, which increases our perplexity about your symptoms. I'd like to redo a few tests and order a spinal tap. I don't want to speculate."

"No," I said adamantly.

Everyone looked at me. Dr. Waterford held my willful gaze with one of his own.

"I doubt that your response is from fear of the procedure," he said, finally.

"What's he talking about, Mom?"

"She knows I suspect either MS or viral encephalitis," Dr. Waterford answered.

"What?" Lynn exclaimed.

I looked at Lynn. Does she think I'm contagious?

"What is viral encephalitis?" Paula said.

"There are three different categories of viruses that can cause encephalitis—common, childhood, and arboviruses," Dr. Waterford said.

"Was she bit by a mosquito or tick on the camping trip?" Dr. Waterford asked Lynn.

"Not that I know of," Lynn said, then to me, "Diana?"

"As far as I know I wasn't bitten, and I don't have any viral infections." I tried not to look at Lynn, but when I took a surreptitious glance, I saw that she was blushing. Thankfully Paula's attention was on the doctor.

"Could my Mom have such a severe reaction to an insect bite so quickly?" Paula asked.

"Given your mom's severe allergy to bees, she could have had an acute response." Dr. Waterford approached my bed. "You can do this, Diana. It's better we know one way or another." He left us alone.

Paula and Lynn turned to me, both trying to mask their fear. I was too exhausted to discuss anything more. I zoned out again.

I felt a caress on my face. A wisp of air accompanied the stroke. The room was dark. A cheek gently brushed against mine. I lay still, not wanting to fully awaken. I absorbed the faint apple scent.

When I felt the bed give, I said, "Don't go."

"You're awake," Lynn said, sounding startled.

"Yes, I thought I was dreaming. It's so good to have you here."

"It's hard. No one wants me to be with you. I miss you."

"Get me out of here," I whispered.

"How, Diana?"

She wiggled her arms around me and pressed her breasts against mine in a provocative hug. Her lips brushed my neck. It was delightful. It was maddening.

The next morning when the breakfast tray arrived, I puzzled over Lynn's visit. Was it real or imagined? Perhaps this whole hospital scene was a dream. My numb legs told me the true story. I dreaded the spinal tap results. The sun's rays warmed the blankets neatly tucked around me. I heard disgruntled voices from the corridor.

"Sh-h-h, ladies! Gentleman! Kindly have your discussion somewhere else. This is a hospital."

Then after more barely audible words, Lynn, Paula, and William entered the room.

"Oh, you're awake," Paula said.

"Just barely," I replied.

"Are you feeling better?" Lynn asked.

"Better?" Had I dreamed Lynn's visit? Was she looking for a general assessment or referring to our illusory embrace? I shook my head and rubbed my temples.

"The doctor will be here soon, love," William said.

He pushed his way around Paula and Lynn to take command. His big sandpapery hands with oversized knuckles tried to grasp mine. I avoided them.

"Dr. Waterford is expected at three," Paula said. She had become quite good at filling me in on past details and upcoming events. The repetition I required didn't bother her.

"What time is it now?" I asked.

"Three," she admitted.

"Doctors are notoriously late," William boomed. "No one else's time matters."

"You should know," Paula retorted.

The bickering that would have erupted was curtailed by the appearance of Dr. Waterford. He looked at William. "We haven't been introduced. You are?"

"Diana's husband," William snapped.

"Good. Everyone is here. Please sit," Dr. Waterford said.

William sat on the radiator under the window, his demeanor a sign that he was either annoyed or bored or that his hemorrhoids were acting up. Lynn and Paula pulled chairs closer to the bed and sat down to face the doctor.

"Diana," Dr. Waterford said, "it's conclusive. You do not have MS or viral encephalitis."

"I don't have MS? I don't have it?" I laughed as relief washed over me. "If I could I would walk on water."

Lynn and Paula jumped up and hugged me. William sat quietly.

"I'm glad to see your optimism," Dr. Waterford said in a serious tone.

"MS or not," William said, "my wife is flat out and nothing you've done has made her better."

"That is true," the doctor said. "Diana's case is puzzling. We've exhausted the search and therefore, the hospital's role."

"She can come home?" Lynn asked.

"Diana, you need 24/7 care and professional observation while we wait for you to progress," Dr. Waterford said. "You also need physical therapy."

"You're waiting for her to get worse?" Paula asked, incredulous.

"Or better, but either way we need to monitor her symptoms," Dr. Waterford said. "Generally it's best to be in a medical care facility. It could be a lengthy recovery."

"Generally?" Paula asked.

"Your support of her is obvious," he said. "However, most often, full time home care is prohibitive because of time and money."

"Money isn't a problem," William said. "I'll see that she gets the proper care."

Dr. Waterford looked at me. "It is your decision."

"I want to go home," I said.

Paula and Lynn flashed a grin. Would they join forces for my well-being?

"Insurance won't cover home care," Dr. Waterford emphasized.

"I don't give a pin about the finances," William said. He glowed when he was gallant. I chose not to point out that his finances were controlled by my company.

"I'll provide a list of equipment and treatment needs. If, after reviewing those, you assure me they can be met, I'll change the arrangements for her release," Dr. Waterford said. "Diana, hospitalized or not, I need to see you every week."

"Yes, of course," I said, ready to agree to anything if it meant my freedom, even though limited. He left the room with William on his heels. I could hear William continue his insistence that he would provide me with the very best of whatever was needed.

Paula and Lynn wanted to plan my homecoming, but I said that I needed to rest. Paula hugged me tightly.

Lynn kissed my forehead and whispered, "See, you are getting out of here."

# CHAPTER NINE

"WELL, LOVE," WILLIAM announced when he entered my room, "I cleaned the place up a might. Nothing too drastic, of course."

"That wasn't necessary, I'm not—" I tried to tell him.

"Anything for you."

"William, I never said I'd be going home with you."

"Of course you're coming home with me, we resolved this yesterday."

"You resolved it for yourself, not for me."

"You're my wife and I'll provide for your care, and it'll be in our home. That's what Dr. Waterford expects."

I did note that he said "our home," but his pseudo chivalry repulsed me.

"I'm going to my apartment," I said. "Dr. Waterford doesn't dictate where I live."

"And what? Ben's going to take care of you?" he retaliated with a laugh. "That little sod hasn't even been in to see you. Has he?"

"I'm returning to the apartment that I just moved into."

"You cannot imagine how much I hate living in the house without you. It's so hollow."

William's desires are the only ones that exist in his world.

"I need to rebuild my health in my own place."

"You're going to need me!" He marched out the door.

"Good-bye, William," I muttered and pulled the sheet over my head.

I wanted to go home so badly, but had I truly considered my needs and the impact on my teenage son, pregnant daughter, and Lynn, a wife and mother of two? For some things like bedpans and sponge baths, a stranger would be far more appropriate than a daughter, or even worse, a son.

"I'VE GOT THE doctor's approval," Paula said when she arrived.

"Are you sure about this?" I asked.

"Absolutely, Mom." There was no doubt evident. I'd evidently done something right as her mother.

"What about the bed?"

"I've made all the arrangements that Dr. Waterford required."

"But how?"

"Mom, you didn't raise dummies. Just relax," she urged.

"Is Ben all right with this?"

"Fine," she said. "He met the delivery company for your bed and he's there now waiting for us."

I dreaded the response but asked, "Has he been to see me?"

"Once, I think. It's rough seeing you like this, Mom."

She busied herself gathering my bags. Her body language seemed in conflict with her words. I probed no deeper.

When Paula and I exited the hospital doors, Lynn ran to greet us, stopping the momentum of my wheelchair with a jolt.

"Diana, Diana," she said breathlessly as she knelt in front of me. "You look good."

I smiled. "You do, too."

We wheeled and walked to Paula's car. The clean air, devoid of hospital smells, was the perfect temperature. The natural daylight brought everything into sharp focus. The old car was like the enchanted coach in Cinderella. My attempts to help Paula and Lynn tuck me into the car seemed only to interfere, so I acceded to their efforts.

"Maybe the seatbelt will help hold you up," Paula said as she pulled it across my upper body and tried to click it. "Oh shit, I'll just tip the seat back. How's that, Mom?"

"Fine, thanks," I said, now at about a 130-degree angle in the front seat.

My son was waiting for us when we arrived at the apartment. His roguish smile gave away his fun-loving and mischievous nature. It was not simply a mother's bias. Ben's impeccable fashion sense, his football-player build, and wavy chestnut brown hair, in addition to the smile, made him a handsome 17 year old. He seemed delighted to lift me up and carry me.

"Do you want to lie on the couch or go to the bedroom?" he asked, slightly panting.

"The bedroom, please," I responded as I searched his face, taking in the features that I knew so well.

For him to carry me in his arms was, while necessary, an awkward shift in our mother and son roles. He set me on the bed. Paula looked at the side rails and tried to release one side.

"I've got it," Ben said, simply pulling up on the rail. "Figured it out before you got here." He beamed.

I beamed back. It was no surprise that William despised my son; Ben's charm upstaged him.

"Do you need anything?" Paula asked.

"A Coke?"

"I'll get it," Lynn said, trying to move quickly from the far side of the bed.

"I've got it," Ben said, already out the door.

Lynn came back to the bed and took my hand. I let her. Paula noticed but didn't say anything.

Ben returned with a small glass of Coke, the tiny bubbles and ice cubes sparkling. Lynn surrendered my hand so I could hold the glass. I took a sip and felt the effervescent beads on my lip and cool tingling in my throat when I swallowed.

"Enough?" Paula asked in a soothing tone. I nodded and she took the glass. "Mom needs to rest."

"You're going to be a wonderful mother," I said.

She smiled at me, then turned to Lynn and Ben. "We need to set up a schedule." She looked at Ben. "Can you give up your parties for one or two nights to stay home with Mom?"

"Shut up," he said, giving her a nudge.

"I'm sorry I've been gone for so long." I saw the blush that bloomed on his neck and face, but the day had exhausted me. I fell asleep.

"DIANA," LYNN SAID, then louder, "Diana?"

I opened my eyes and saw that Lynn had a tray in her hands.

"I thought you should eat," Lynn said as she set the tray on a table beside the bed.

I touched her arm. "Thank you."

"I'm so glad you're home," she said.

She took the bed controls in her hand and stared at the buttons. She pressed one and it raised the foot. "Oops, guess that's not it." She pushed again and it lowered, then tried another button and the head raised.

"That's good," I said to stop her button pushing before I became seasick.

The door was closed. The apartment was quiet.

"Where are Paula and Ben?" I asked.

I've got 7 to 10:30. Paula went home and Ben said he would be back by 8."

"What time is it now?" I asked.

"8:30," she replied. "Ben was out the door the minute you fell asleep."

"Well, now that I'm home we can sort this out. He's not used to his mother being debilitated."

I picked up the spoon. "The soup looks delicious."

The first sip was warm, wet, and the slippery noodles soothed my throat. What dripped from the spoon Lynn would dab with a napkin. Her delicate pats were charming but out of character. It made dribbling worthwhile. She considered the mess I was making and took the spoon. I smiled. I had missed her. Was she happy?

I tried to ignore the pressure building in my head and pay attention to Lynn's verbal deluge.

"I'm in this with you. We'll stick this out together. I'll help take care of you. I've been so worried. I'd have stayed with you but Paula insisted that you would want me to hold things together at work. William said my presence at the hospital was inappropriate, that you were his responsibility. And Dick wanted me home to recuperate from our ordeal."

"Are you OK? I mean, have you recovered?" I asked.

"I went back to work as soon as I could. What else was I to do? I wasn't family so I couldn't see you in the ICU. Until you were moved to another room, the only place to find out about you was at work through Paula or William."

"I'm so sorry." The headache was intensifying, but I didn't want her to feel neglected now. "I hope that my being home will be easier for you."

She kissed my cheek.

I wrapped my arms around her. "I know that so far it's better for me. You're here, the soup was good, and the bed works." I wanted to keep her there forever.

I wanted to be with her but the pressure and pain in my head made me want to sleep. "Can I have something for my headache?"

She handed me two pills from one of the prescription bottles on the dresser.

"I'm very tired," I said. "Will you be OK?"

"Yeah, I brought some work from the office. Trying to win brownie points with the boss." She grinned but then turned serious. "But, Diana, we haven't been able to really talk and we need to. There are so many questions."

I brought her hand to my lips and kissed it. Lynn was here and asking questions. That was a good sign, wasn't it?

I woke with excruciating pain in my head. I was disoriented and weak. The soup had run its course.

"Please, help," I whispered.

Lynn, who had been sitting in the corner on an old rocking chair, startled me as she vaulted upward and raced to the bed.

"Diana, are you all right? What can I do? What do you need?"

"Do you see a bed pan?" I asked.

Lynn shook her head and yelled, "Ben, your mother needs help to get to the bathroom."

The pressure in my bladder seemed to increase rapidly, quickly making the situation urgent.

"Is he coming?" I said, pulling on the bed rail, squirming toward the edge of the bed. "I'm so sorry. I hate being so much trouble."

Sleepy and rubbing his eyes, Ben entered the bedroom.

"You're no trouble, Mom. It's OK," he said, lowering the rail. "I'll just carry you." And he swooped me up in his arms.

"Please hurry," I said. "Can you just set me on the toilet?"

Ben returned for me and carried me back to the bed. He raised the bed rail when I was settled.

"Thank you, son. Get some sleep, you have school tomorrow."

Ben smiled at me. "You sound like my mom."

"I love you, Ben. I'm sorry this is happening."

He headed to the door and when he got there, turned around. "I love you too, Mom. Good night."

After he was gone I perused the room. "Is there a bedpan?"

"Do you need to go again?" Lynn asked, wide-eyed.

"No, future reference," I said. "I don't want to wear diapers and I don't want to be more of a burden than I am already."

"It's OK. I said I'd do anything, and I meant that."

"I appreciate it, Lynn," I said. "I saw a bedpan flower pot once. Maybe if I imagine my backside tickled by flowers the ordeal would be more tolerable."

Lynn held up a stainless steel bedpan. "This is all we've got for now."

# CHAPTER TEN

THE NEXT DAY Paula entered bearing a basket full of candies, flowers, and books from the employees.

"How wonderful," I said. "Thank everyone for me."

"Of course." She noticed my current hairstyle. "Pulling your hair out this morning?"

That was probably an accurate assessment, as I'd fingered and pressed it to death. "The pain in my head."

"Got something for that," she said, setting the bounty down on the bed. "Talked to Dr. Waterford this morning. It's another drug, supposedly stronger."

"Anything," I said, reaching for the capsule and the water she had retrieved from the table. As grateful as I was for the pills, they only eased a trace of the pain.

With more enticing foods and longer private times with people I cared about, things were better. Paula, Lynn, and Ben helped me do physical therapy routines. I was making progress. I managed a couple of steps, could sit up more and enjoyed a few wheelchair excursions to the grounds around the apartment complex. The outpatient nurse came to check on my condition. I was surprised by the quality of the questions my son and daughter asked. They took their roles very seriously. Someone was always with me.

William's duty was dinner. His theatrical unveiling of what he brought made the rest of his visit bearable. The wine was always first out of the bag. He would raise the bottle up for my inspection and nod of approval. He'd smile, uncork, and pour two glasses, taking just a sip from his glass as a taste. Then one more swig for good measure. Since I could only sniff the glass, he would finish the bottle. Dinner typically consisted of course upon course of fine cuisine packed in a box. He would natter on while we ate about the incompetence of employees who made his life difficult. I would try to steer his attention back to the food. He would leave right after we finished our meal.

Steve and Kathleen came often. It gave me a chance to hear Steve's take on William's new sense of importance and the danger that he might unleash in my absence. Kathleen would bring a healthy and surprisingly delicious baked goodie. She brought the most decadent-looking chocolate cake once and told me it had pureed beets in the batter. She wanted me to eat beets after she discovered they help increase blood flow to the brain. I thought it would taste awful, but it was scrumptious. Lynn and Paula wouldn't even try it. Lynn didn't eat desserts and Paula didn't touch vegetables. Ben and I were happy not to share.

I was ready to get back to the office. With the walker, the wheelchair, and my support team it was feasible. I needed to assess the company climate and reassure both staff and the board. It was time.

I was in bed, running scenarios on how I could convince Paula, Lynn, and Dr. Waterford of my plan, when suddenly my stomach muscles constricted.

"Ah-h-h-h-h," I gasped as I doubled over.

"What the hell is going on?" Ben asked, appearing bedside.

"I don't know," I said, moaning.

Ben tried to help me straighten from my curled position. It was as though my body had snapped shut like a roly-poly bug. My body wouldn't unfold.

He locked the bedrail in place and ran down the hall shouting, "I'm calling Paula!"

I heard him say, "Paula, it's Mom, she's doubled over and won't stop groaning, I don't know what to do."

The next I knew they were both in my bedroom.

"What happened? Paula asked.

"She was all bent over. I couldn't straighten her." Ben's voice quavered.

"I'm OK now," I said and tried to tell Paula, "It's all right. I'm sorry you had to come over."

"Mom, we're here for you," she said.

"Guess I have something new to share with Dr. Waterford," I said.

Brother and sister exchanged a worried glance.

"It better not be another mystery symptom he can't solve," Ben exclaimed, then muttered, "Not on my watch." He left the room.

Paula stayed for several hours, but there was no recurrence. Was this a fluke or yet another symptom? I tried to pass it off as indigestion and told her I needed to get back to the office, maybe just a little each day.

"Indigestion, my foot," she retorted. "We don't need something like that to happen when you're at the office."

Paula kissed me and went to talk to Ben. I could hear them in the living room. I wanted to cook, clean, and take care of my children. Instead they were caring for me.


I WAS GRATEFUL for Lynn's appearance at six. She closed the bedroom door and placed a small white, red, and yellow bag on a chair. She gathered my hands in hers.

"Up to new tricks, are you?" she asked, moving closer to give me a hug. Paula had obviously filled her in.

"Guess so," I said, holding on tight to her embrace. As I relaxed, the fear I had held in check released with a shudder.

"Is it happening again?" she asked in a loud, urgent voice.

"No, I'm OK," I reassured her. There was a knock at the door.

"Is everything OK?" Ben asked.

"Yes, false alarm, thanks," Lynn said.

I tried to pull her close again but she moved away. We both blushed.

"How was work?" I asked.

"Nothing runs smoothly without you. Production is putting out unacceptable product. Sometimes 50 percent rework.

Inventory is short on components. We've had to ship Express Air."

"Lynn, slow down."

She didn't pay attention and went on. "Paula said not to bother you with this stuff. We're all doing our best. There are customer complaints. People are scared about your health, about the company, and about their jobs."

"I've talked with Paula about my coming into the office. She wouldn't hear of it. You may have to help me get there."

"I don't want to go against Paula," Lynn said. "She is trying very hard to maintain order in the office and do what's best for you. She loves you very much."

"And you?" I asked.

"Oh, absolutely I want what's best. You know that."

I had hoped she would say that she loved me, too. Could Lynn care for me so much and not be interested in an intimate relationship? In my state how could I ask? And what did it matter?

I took her hand and stroked it, then laced my fingers with hers and squeezed tenderly.

"I want you back," she said. "You make everything better."

I laughed. Her smiling face drew me. I stared deep into her eyes, trying to touch her mind and extract the answers I craved.

"What are you looking for?" she said, staring back at me.

"Nothing," I said, then pointed to the bag on the chair. "What did you bring?"

"Oh! It's probably ruined." She opened the Dairy Queen bag and pulled out a melting sundae. With stacks of napkins, she tried to soak up the dripping ice cream.

"Where's your dessert?" I asked between hurried spoonfuls.

"I ate at home," she said.

"How is home, Lynn? Are Dick and the boys all right?"

"They're a little annoyed about my being gone so much. I'm just not capable of dealing with their everyday needs right now. But they try to understand. I'm a bit of a nervous wreck."

"Lynn, you've got to unwind. Take a walk. Play some racquetball. This isn't good for you."

"Of course it isn't, but my partner isn't up to a game these days." She dropped her head down to rest on the bed. I put the ice cream container and napkins on the sheets and placed my hands, melted ice cream and all, on each side of her head. I tried to massage her but strands of hair clung to my sticky fingers. I tried to disentangle. Lynn joined in the effort. Her hair was a mess. I laughed as we moistened tissues to remove the gooey ice cream. She was a sight. Being good natured and not having seen herself, she joined in my laughter. The tissues shredded even more. Lynn gave up and got a washcloth from the bathroom.

I hated napping when Lynn was there. But I had to succumb each evening. She'd wake me 30 minutes before she had to leave. Usually she would help me get to the bathroom for my final pit stop. When I was safely in bed, we'd share a long hug and caress each other. Then she would go, leaving the door open so Ben could hear if I needed anything.

This evening it was not Lynn's soft touch that woke me, but the sharp pull of contracting muscles. It was as intense as the first occurrence. Lynn sprang up.

"Ben," she yelled. "It's happening again."

He came to the door, fear on his sleepy face. He stood by the bed, and we waited, our eyes locked. Was it over? I managed to take a deep breath before my muscles constricted again. Ben tried to keep me from folding but my body clamped shut.

"Go call my sister," he growled at Lynn.

There was hardly any rest between the episodes. I took short gulps of air as though in labor and tried to brace myself for the next contraction.

Ben went from the front door to the bedroom. Lynn whimpered and paced beside the bed.

Paula rushed through the door. "Dr. Waterford said he'll meet us at the ER."

DR. WATERFORD DID not need to consult the chart in his hands to see the deterioration. He pushed my head upright, looked into my eyes, and watched as my head fell back to the original position upon his release.

He clasped my hands. "Nothing adds up. Your nerves and brain are not responding to the medications." He turned to include Paula and Ben. "I'll have her re-admitted, repeat all the tests, and order another MRI for comparison."

The next days were a blur. The meds allowed me to sleep between the seizures. Dr. Waterford tried first one medication and then another. At times I would take 14 medications twice daily. If the medication minimized the seizures, then the side effects or my allergic reactions would necessitate its being discontinued.

Any sense of control I had regained was stripped away: first physical debilitation, then mental impairment, and now drugged oblivion and involuntary convulsions. Soon after the tests, I was moved from the hospital to a medical care facility. Dr. Waterford said it was highly specialized for rehabilitation and treatment of cerebrally impaired individuals.

"They can meet your needs best," he said. "You must realize, Diana, your condition is unique."

The brain lesions qualified me to be on the brain damage ward. Once at the facility that diagnosis became a horrific reality.

At dinner, the wheelchair brigade met in the cafeteria. I was wheeled between two ladies with tubes protruding from their throats. The gurgling sounds, the whish-who, whish-who of respirators, made me close my eyes so as not to see my future. I struggled to block the noises. My heart beat faster and faster. Straining to control myself, I made my muscles rigid until they shook, then my hands whipped out. I opened my eyes to see my plate slide across the table and sail through the air until it collided with the back of a chair. The occupant never flinched. I was grateful I didn't behead anyone!

How was it possible that I was here? What did I do or
fail to do that I deserved this? I had to get better. But how
in the hell could I eat meals when others are regurgitating?
Their surgical head scars weren't covered. They didn't talk,
they gurgled and hissed. How could I be so callous about
their circumstances, so intolerant of the noises generated by
life-sustaining equipment and severely ill people? I repulsed
myself. There was no excuse for my abhorrence, nor could I
control it. I was panic-stricken.

An attendant went to clean the mess, while another came to
me.

"What happened? Are you OK?" he asked.

"I can't," I whispered, trying to wheel away, then cried, "I
can't eat like this. I need out of here."

"I've got her," Paula's voice rang out.

My wheelchair moved backward at a pace that would have
deposited me on the floor had I not been buckled in.

"I'm so sorry," Paula said when we were safely in my room.

"Don't be sorry," I said. "You didn't do anything wrong."

"I saw the patients in the cafeteria. You can't go back there.
You're not like them. You're going to get better."

"Paula, are you sure?"

We both cried, too terrified to face the answer.


PAULA SHOWED UP every morning and brought breakfast
from Waffle House and then returned with dinner. She was
occasionally relieved by William.

Dr. Waterford ordered counseling sessions for me. I got advice
on how to help my children, friends, and business associates deal
with my illness. Neither the medical nor the psychological help
was giving me my life back or any hope of it.

Days and days passed with no diagnosis. Treatments were
geared toward trying to preserve my body's abilities and keep
pain at a bearable level. Dr. Waterford never wavered in his
pursuit of an answer. He stressed optimism as a key to healing,

and personally examined each change in my condition. I was a yoyo, physically, mentally, and emotionally.

There were days I could write memos and letters or sign documents. Between Paula's attentiveness to the company and her devotion to me, we managed to keep the board members, employees, and clients satisfied. Often I was in a spasm, up-chucking, itching from a rash, or unconscious. My appetite dropped and as I shrank to preteen size, I blended into the rehab population. I'd slowly get better, only to come crashing back down harder than before.

I was ashamed to be seen. Paula controlled my visitors. She acted as my sentry. William and Lynn were exceptions. She couldn't monitor their stops. Parker was slipped in a couple of times for a romp in my room. Kathleen dropped in occasionally.

I had a wheelchair, walker, and cane readily available for my changing needs. I tried to keep fighting, but every crash whittled away my determination. I focused my unbearable frustration into relentless physical therapy workouts when I could. It was a sad replacement for racquetball.

When I allowed myself to face how incapacitated I had become, despair crept in. My success and survival had depended upon my dauntless courage to shape my life's path. It was time I considered an exit plan. I would not surrender my dignity.

I had heard of Dr. Kavorkian, but assisted suicide had not been a topic of interest to this aspiring and resolute woman entrepreneur. Now I regretted not being more knowledgeable. My resources were limited. I knew not to approach Paula, and talking to Lynn was prohibitive because of her religion. I couldn't tell what Dr. Waterford's position would be. Very few doctors were sympathetic to requests for dying with dignity.

Why should I face life so broken? Did I have to hide another crucial secret? How could I die with dignity without saying goodbye to those I love? I was surrounded by people so I knew I had to be successful the first time. I considered pills. I certainly had access and I could hoard them. But which ones? How many would be enough? If I could talk to other patients, perhaps I could find out. But if I spoke to the wrong one or waited too long, it would no longer be up to me. Though at the moment it seemed I was better, I wasn't fooled.

# CHAPTER ELEVEN

"DIANA, YOU'VE MADE significant advances," Dr. Waterford said as he started the conference with Paula, Lynn and I.

I thought, how can wheelchair to bed to wheelchair be significant progress? But before I could say my words of despair out loud, he said, "You're ready for a couple of brief outings."

"What?" I exclaimed.

"I'll take her," Lynn said and gripped the wheelchair handles, ready to push me out of there.

Paula stopped our departure with a glare at Lynn. "What do you mean by brief? What restrictions?"

"Diana, you're still in recovery but I think you need fresh air and stimulation from the real world," he answered.

"You're right, I need to get out," I said. "My body is enough of a prison."

"How about four hours tomorrow and then another four hours in a couple of days?" Dr. Waterford asked.

Lynn and Paula excused themselves and hurriedly moved into the hallway. I could see them murmuring to each other, Day-Timers out.

"Why not today?" I asked with urgency. I was afraid this chance would vanish if I didn't immediately act.

"You have special needs to prepare for; use today to plan for tomorrow," he responded. "If all goes well and you don't have any more setbacks, your release will be soon."

I was ecstatic. "My new mantra is regulate, balance, and pace. I say it to myself when I feel anxiety building."

He actually smiled. "I wish all my patients were as determined to get well."

LYNN BEAMED AS we wheeled down the hallway of the rehab center on the way back to my room. "It's you and me tomorrow," she said, bouncing with each step. "What do you want to do?"

"You mean it's already been decided?"

Lynn stopped just short of my room.

"Do I have any say in this plan?" I asked.

"Of course."

When we got to the room, I spun the chair around so that Lynn and I could face each other. Her eyes reflected confusion.

"I've been hoping, dreaming, and planning to get out of this place." I stroked her cheek, noticing that I had more sensitivity in my fingers. "These outings are critical to me."

"Don't you want to go with me?" Lynn asked softly.

"Of course."

"What's wrong then?"

"This place regulates everything. I can't even take a pee without someone measuring it. It's my life, but so many others control it. Can't I have some control or at least an opinion?"

"Paula and I decided that we need a schedule since we have to coordinate work and make sure there is appropriate transportation. I have the first outing because I'm more available right now, and I know what you need. I thought you'd be happy." Her expression was apprehensive.

"Lynn, I'm thrilled it's you and me."

Her look cleared and she wrapped her arms around me in a tight hug before she helped me to bed.

Tired, I lay down. "What is my outing schedule?"

"Paula has a situation at the company, but you're not to worry," Lynn said. "She needs to resolve it before she can take any more time away. We thought Kathleen would want to take you to lunch or tea. I thought we could go to the park tomorrow and have a picnic."

"I'd love a picnic. Can we have Kentucky Fried Chicken?" I did relish the idea of time just with her, but I also felt the pull of my neglected work responsibilities. "If we make an appearance at the office I could also do some work before we'd have to come back."

"OK. This is going to be great. Should I get wine?" Lynn asked.

Shivers ran along my spine in anticipation, but I had to say, "With all my medications, I'm afraid the wine is out for me, Lynn."

"Oh, you're right. That was silly."

By the end of visiting hours, we had packed the next day with grandiose potential. I wanted to sit under the vast blue sky by a tree, so I could savor the musky scents of the leaf-cluttered ground, listen to the wind, and watch the birds.

Too excited to sleep, I thought about Dr. Waterford's words. If these excursions proved to help heal my body, then I could be released from this place soon. It would be wise not to return exhausted, regardless of how much I wanted to do.

Morning brought Paula with breakfast from McDonalds. I patted her belly. She was pregnant from a man she was living with, who I did not think she loved. I wanted her to find romance and happiness, but had not set a great example.

"Are you taking time for yourself?"

She nodded, tracing her belly too. "What are you and Lynn up to today?"

"A picnic," I replied.

"You'll love that, I'm sure. Not too far, I hope?"

"No, not far," I said. "You really will be a good mother."

"I hope so," Paula said.

Lynn stood in the doorway. "Ready?"

I smiled my hello to her.

Paula stood. "Will I see you at the office later?"

"Yes, we'll be there after lunch." I glanced at Lynn to confirm. She nodded.

Paula left us. Lynn gave me a sweet kiss on the cheek. "Are you excited?"

"Are you kidding? Let's get out of here!"

Lynn took control of my wheels and pushed me to her jeep, which was parked in a handicapped space. Much time had passed since I was last in the jeep. My life had moved from the fast track to a wheelchair. Now I was in the passenger seat, a metaphor for most aspects of my current life. Tears flowed: the reservoir had opened.

Lynn looked over. "What's wrong?"

"I'm just feeling emotional."

"Are you OK?"

"I don't know. Let's just go."

Lynn put the car in gear and drove.

"The fried chicken smells wonderful," I said. "Do we have to wait?"

"Go ahead."

I opened the lid of the bucket and took a big whiff. I plucked a wing and took a bite of the meatiest part. My taste buds felt as though they were doing a little dance in my mouth.

Lynn looked over and laughed. "I'm glad to see you enjoying that."

"Do you want a piece?" I asked.

I wiped greasy chicken from my lips and returned her smile. Thoughts of food disappeared. I looked at her silhouetted features.

"Not right now," she said, her attention back on the road.

Sun rays filtered through her hair and splintered into delicate threads of light. I was captivated.

"We're here," Lynn announced. "Are you up for a walk?"

"Sure." I hadn't been aware that we had arrived.

Opening the jeep door, I inhaled deeply, then coughed from the rush of crisp air. I took in a clear breath and proclaimed, "Fabulous."

Lynn and I exchanged silly grins like naughty schoolgirls who had cut class. She got out and moved to the back of the jeep.

"Cane or wheelchair?" she asked.

The well-maintained path took a moderate slope as it descended into a valley, where a stout wooden bridge spanned a narrow ravine. Here the trail split and wandered upward out of sight.

In consideration of the distance, I said, "The wheelchair, I think, but I'll carry the cane for later. I can hold the lunch and blanket, too, if you'll take control of the chair."

"Love to."

Wheeling on the gravel path was a challenge, but we were soon on the bridge and able to peer down at the babbling brook. I watched the gentle flow of water as it passed under us and out of sight. Could I shrink myself and set sail on a leaf and escape?

Lynn, who was not as reflective, spun the chair to point it toward a concrete table. "Is that table OK?"

I said yes, it was a lovely setting and I was hungry. I could go back to the bridge later.

"Good," she said and pushed me to the picnic table.

We ate the chicken, potatoes, rolls, and corn right from the packages. The soda, although a far cry from wine, was good with the crispy, crunchy coating on the chicken.

The dormant grasses, brush, and trees exhibited their winter hues in grays and browns, their fragrance masked by the lunch aromas. A rush of energy charged through me. Could I have hope? Was this moment enough of a reason to go on living?

I reached my hand across the table to touch Lynn's. "Thank you. This is even better than I had hoped."

She popped up, ran around the end of the table, and straddled the bench to sit next to me. She took my hand and kissed it. I raised hers and slowly licked her fingertips and kissed each one. She pulled her hand free, threw both arms around me, and squeezed hard. It was an embrace that I wished would last forever.

I lay my head on her shoulder and snuggled into her neck. My breathing was deep and slow, my muscles relaxed. It wasn't until she straightened that I realized the weight she must have borne.

She stroked my face and leaned forward. I closed my eyes in anticipation of our first intimate kiss. Our lips met and desire rose. I slid urgent hands under Lynn's bra. I massaged her breast and felt her nipple harden. She shivered and I pulled her closer. Suddenly awareness that we were in a public place filtered through, and we let go of each other reluctantly, as though pulling magnets apart.

I decided to spend the last of our time together on the bridge rather than stop at the office. I practiced reciting my mantra: regulate, balance, pace.

My attempt to wheel myself up the gravel path proved to be more arduous than the workout I did on the gym equipment. Lynn had to help me on the uphill climb. Together we made it back to the jeep.

Paula came that evening with dinner. "I thought you were going to stop by the office today?"

"We ran out of time," I said.

"She took you too far, didn't she?"

"No, the park was just a few minutes into the hills. It was the perfect place."

"Well, everyone was hoping to see you. The office looked really nice."

"I'm sorry," I said, realizing that she had made special efforts and was hurt. "I decided that to be outside on my first excursion was better for me than to spend my time out of rehab at the office."

"Well," she reluctantly agreed, "perhaps you're right."

"Paula," I began urgently, "I want out of this damn horrible place. I don't want to crash and land on my ass again."

"Mom, oh Mom," she cried, "I know. This is just so hard."

"Tell me what's going on."

"There's no crisis or anything. We just cleaned up and were looking forward to you coming in. It's been a long time. I thought you'd want to see everything and everyone. You used to live, eat, and sleep for Pioneering."

"That's true."

Why hadn't I gone in to work? Was it fear of a relapse? Had this moderation stuff really sunk in and transformed me? Paula was waiting for a response. Dare I think out loud?

"This has changed my perspective on life," I said carefully. "I've been told that I'm going to have to set my expectations lower, stay flexible, and listen to my body."

"Do you mean that you don't know about coming back to the office?" she asked with a deep frown.

"Pages of my life have been ripped out and I'm afraid to make plans for the future. Does that make any sense?"

"Honestly, no," she said. "Not from you."

"In some aspects I'm more clear than I've ever been before. In other ways I'm more confused." I was half amazed and half disturbed to hear my own words.

"Let's just leave it at that," Paula said in exasperation, ready to leave. "Maybe we'll see you after your lunch with Kathleen."

I pondered how my thoughts felt deeper and how my ability to express those complicated thoughts was more limited. Language is a great tool. Truth could be revealed or obscured just by a person's choice of words.

# CHAPTER TWELVE

KATHLEEN ARRIVED FOR our lunch date two days later. She was punctual as always and gave me a gentle squeeze. "I've been looking forward to taking you to lunch."

"Me, too. I'm ready." I was in the wheelchair with my cane on my lap. I was no longer an inexperienced traveler.

"Do I push?"

"Two choices as I see it. Either hop on board or push."

She smiled. "Push was more what I had in mind. Glad to see you haven't lost your sense of humor."

Each time I went outside, even in the wheeled contraption, I gulped fresh air. I envied a hummingbird that zipped toward a flower and a fuzzy-tailed red squirrel that sat on his hind legs munching a nut at the base of a pine tree.

A constant challenge for a disabled person without special wheelchair equipment was getting in and out of cars. My hope was that I wouldn't require such equipment long term. After I was in the car, Kathleen fumbled to load the wheelchair. I gave her some dismantling tips and we were off.

Kathleen had chosen The Blue House Restaurant. It was in an old gingerbread house with a white wooden porch graced with curlicue architectural details. Fortunately it had modern-day wheelchair accessibility. The dining was formal. The waitress moved a chair to make room for me at the table. Warm cracked-wheat bread and honey-butter was served before we were fully settled. We had to select from the three entree choices. The muscles in my back began to twitch. I tried to forcibly stop the jerks. I took a few deep breaths as I had been instructed in biofeedback. The waitress appeared at our table.

"What would you like to order?"

I looked at her sudden appearance and lost my train of thought.

"Are you all right?" Kathleen asked, reaching for my hand.

"Trying to be."

Kathleen waved the waitress away. "What's wrong?"

"Spasms. I hate this."

"Is there anything I can do?"

"No, there's nothing anyone can do. I'm popping medication that's supposed to help. The physical therapist suggested deep breathing." I tried to draw another breath as several muscles twisted sharply. My back was forced into an arch and my attempt to inhale was cut short. The seizure finally passed. "My body feels like it's being squeezed in a vise."

"Diana, I'm so sorry. Do you want me to take you to the car? Should I take you back?"

"The car would be less embarrassing."

By the time we arrived at the car, my arms were exhausted from struggling to remain upright in the wheelchair.

She opened the car door and helped support my weight as I shifted from the wheelchair to the seat. I fell back, my muscles writhing. I heard her load the wheelchair, then slam the trunk closed. She got in the driver's seat and looked at me.

"Should I take you back?" she asked.

I was perspiring with the effort to direct my body to relax, which failed. I stole quick short breaths when I could.

"Not yet. It'll stop," I said through clenched teeth.

I could see her white-knuckle grip on the steering wheel.

When the seizures finally released me, I lay still for a few minutes to collect myself. Kathleen handed me a tissue to wipe the drops of perspiration that rolled down my face. I noticed her face was streaked with tears. My clothes stuck to my body and I was exhausted.

"It's like a terrible force of nature takes me over and there is nothing I can do about it," I whispered.

I began to tremble and cry, as did Kathleen. We sat in silence until our tears subsided, now woven together in a bond of compassionate humanity.

On the ride back to the rehab center, my mind raced. How would the seizure affect Dr. Waterford's judgment about my outings? Was this my last one? How could I stand the rehab asylum much longer? The closer we got, the more desperate and erratic my thoughts became.

Kathleen wheeled me straight to my room. She steadied me as I got into bed.

"This is very difficult for me," I said. "In an instant my life changed. I went from being a capable, take-charge woman to a totally helpless one. I don't know how to cope."

"Diana, you need to rest."

"Kathleen," I said with as much urgency as I could muster. She looked at me and our eyes locked. "Can I trust that what I share with you is in confidence?"

"Yes, of course."

"Things that were never important to me before are now. The doctor claims I need to learn to tone down my life. Paula feels I've lost my business zeal. I truly don't know how to live a life that's so unpredictable and out of my control."

"Oh," she said. That one word, so simplistic yet it might mean "I totally understand" or "I don't get it."

I tried a different angle. "I've never thought about dying before this ordeal."

"You're not dying, Diana."

"Maybe not this minute, but the life I had is dead. There have been times I couldn't wipe my own butt. I hate not having control of my life. I'm terrified of being a research specimen, manipulated and having with no say. There's no quality in this kind of living. There's no grace."

"No," she agreed. "I've always admired the gusto you put into things. Nothing is just black and white for you. It's got to be full-spectrum color and animated."

I decided to go for it. "If I choose to end this unbearable way of being, will you help me?"

The color drained from her face. She stared at me, then paced the room. I waited. She stood beside the bed as still as a statue, as white as the finest Carrara marble.

"It hurts me to see you like this. I don't know what I would do if it was me. I will help you in any way I can, but I must talk to Steve."

Kathleen's words punctured the fog of fatigue and shame that settles over me after a seizure. All I could do was nod. She turned and left the room.


LATE MORNING, KATHLEEN appeared. Her normal glow had returned and she walked in with purpose.

"I wanted to check on you," she said, looking me over and then handing me a beautiful lavender envelope. "Please read this." She walked to the door. "I'll take it with me when I go."

The card showed two women dressed in white with purple trimmed ornate dresses, sipping tea on a wrought-iron bench in a garden gazebo. "Read," she instructed as she checked the hallway before closing the door. She gave my shoulder a pat, then paced as I read.

> *Steve and I talked when I got home. It was hard seeing you like that. I've struggled with what you said, and do not know if I understood. Let me apologize now if I am mistaken. I do not want to offend or suggest anything you have not asked. If it is your desire that Steve and I obtain literature on dying with dignity, we will do so. It is best none of us talk about these issues. We ask you to give it three months. You must listen and do everything the doctors say. If, and I do mean if, the time comes, we will step in on your behalf. Meanwhile, you must not give up. If this is your wish, please indicate.*

When I finished reading, I nodded. She had pen in hand. I signed and dated the card. She tucked it away and hugged me.

"Please get better. We love you."

"Yes, thank you. Thank you so much. You are a dear friend."

Goals and deadlines I could deal with. Three months seemed like a long, long time, but Kathleen had lifted my desperation about sinking uncontrollably into useless vegetation forever. Her requests were reasonable.

The next morning Paula burst into my room. "Mom, last night on a news program, they warned about six drugs you should never take under any circumstances. I know that you're on three of them. We've got to do something. This is dangerous."

"Paula, take a breath. Remember the devastation from the other drugs. Whatever I'm on now, I'm functional, getting stronger even."

"There's got to be another way. The side effects are terrible." She held out her highlighted notes for me to read.

I took the paper from her and scanned the scribbling.

"Mom, we've got to do something."

"Like what?"

"I don't know. You're better, but you're not fixed."

"You're right," I said. "But it isn't from lack of effort. They've tried everything. Even things you say they never should have."

"But Mom?"

"But what?"

"They have to try harder. This isn't fair."

"Life isn't fair, Paula."

She looked at me as though I had just vanquished a cardinal truth, which I had done. I had taught her that with enough determination and effort, you could overcome anything in life.

"My first son dying after only 48 hours wasn't fair," I continued. "Your father going to Vietnam and returning so haunted with nightmares that he threatened to kill us wasn't fair. What my dad did to me, my brother, and sisters wasn't fair."

"Mom!" She placed her hands flat on the bedspread as though to stop me.

"Maybe I've been wrong all this time," I said. "Maybe my whole life has been pointless. Struggle, struggle, struggle only to have everything I've achieved deflated like a pierced balloon. The air rushes out and leaves behind a useless piece of rubber. This might be as good as I get, and maybe the drugs will kill me, but it's all I've got right now."

"Don't. It hasn't been pointless. I need you. My baby will need you. The news scared me. I keep wanting to do more and I can't. I don't know what or how." She grabbed me in a bear hug and we wept.

"You have a new life inside you," I whispered. "You have taken extraordinary care of me. You have so much more to experience in this life."

The sound of a throat clearing broke our embrace. Dr. Waterford, in his lab coat, watched from the doorway as we parted.

"How are you this morning?" he asked, then acknowledged Paula with a nod.

"Paula heard a disconcerting news report about the danger of taking some of the drugs I'm on," I said.

"You've had such adverse reactions to certain medications that the choice of what to prescribe became very limited," he said. "However, with the progress you've made currently, we must stay the course."

Paula and I remained silent. He glanced between us. "Have you enjoyed your outings?"

"Yes, very much," I said.

His gaze went to Paula who gave him a slight nod. "I understand it's your birthday tomorrow."

"I forgot," I said in surprise.

"Since the party is at your house," he said, "the guest of honor should be there."

I was speechless and Paula had a very big grin on her face.

"There is one condition that is not negotiable, Diana," Dr. Waterford continued. "You must see a mental health therapist once a week. Do you agree?"

He wasn't talking about an outing, he meant I could go home. "Yes! Yes! Yes!"

I was beyond relief that I had been with Kathleen when I had the seizure. Her discretion got me out of here. I was going home.

# CHAPTER THIRTEEN

PAULA WAS NEVER late. But today of all days she was not here. I waited. My mind darted from worry about my overburdened, pregnant daughter to the urgency I felt to get away from the sounds and smells of human frailty and approaching death. My secret agreement with Kathleen gave me a sense of resolve; ultimately I would be in control of my life. Now I had to live it to the best of my ability, or not.

Paula and Lynn arrived. Paula erupted, listing the morning fires she had to put out.

"Take a breath. You're here now." Paula and Lynn exchanged a glance. "Tell me."

"Your apartment . . ." She hesitated.

"Tell me."

"Ben needs some time."

"Some time?" I asked.

"It's complicated."

I glanced at Lynn to see if she would reveal more, but she remained silent.

"What does he need time for?"

"He's lost your apartment."

"What do you mean he's lost our apartment? How could he lose my home?" I exclaimed. Then I saw her familiar look of stubborn protectiveness. "What are you covering up for your brother?"

Paula sighed. "The apartment manager kicked him out for having too many loud parties."

I stared at her and Lynn. They did not look back.

"Where were you going to take me?" I asked, incredulous.

Paula went on as though she didn't hear me. "Ben's pleading with the manager to let you stay if he leaves. He's supposed to call to let us know."

"I can't believe he's been that irresponsible."

Paula ignored my comment and added another surprise revelation. "You could stay with me. But with Jamie and the dogs you wouldn't have much privacy or space."

"What do you mean, Jamie?" I said.

Paula answered as though I should know. "He's the baby's father so I decided to live with him."

"You're welcome at my house," Lynn said.

"How long have you known about Ben?" I asked her, the chaos of the situation making me feel churlish and helpless again.

Paula's cell phone rang.

Lynn patted my shoulder and whispered, "I just found out."

I squeezed her hand and held it until Paula got off the phone.

"Ben signed an agreement that he would not be on the premises and the manager relented," she said.

"Where is Ben going?" I asked.

"He's moving in with his friend Trent."

"I should have made arrangements with Trent's family at the beginning of this disaster."

"You had enough to deal with," Lynn said. "His father could have taken some responsibility."

"Now the issue is how can we manage without Ben?" Paula interjected.

"She can stay with us," Lynn said.

Paula ignored Lynn. "We're really only one person short but he would have been there through the night."

"I can move around the apartment on my own," I added. "It might feel good to do some cooking."

Lynn and Paula exchanged a dubious look.

"I'll stay with her," Lynn offered.

"Like move in?" Paula asked. "What about Dick?"

"I'll tell him it's doctors' orders and that it's just until we can arrange something else," Lynn said.

I saw conflicting emotions on Paula's face. I tried to read Lynn's. Was her offer prompted by intimate feelings for me or as a shareholder with obligations to the company? I had to stop this merry-go-round; the stress could set off another seizure.

"Let's go to lunch," I said.

"Good idea," Paula said. "We have to wait for Ben's all-is-clear call. His friends are helping him pack and move."

"That's the least they can do," Lynn said.

I ignored Paula's death glare toward Lynn. She was right, but he was my son, a teenage boy, and I should have been taking care of him. His friend's family were good people. He would be safe.

When we got to the apartment it was surprisingly neat. Ben had vacuumed and dusted. I would miss him. I was relieved that he wasn't saddled with caring for his invalid mother, but also concerned about the impact my debilitation was having on him.

A few people from the office appeared at the door for my birthday party. Paula gave out birthday hats and whistles. Dick, Lynn's husband showed up. William came with several bottles of wine. Steve and Kathleen arrived. Kathleen had made a triple-layer birthday cake. Paula saw to that. I only had to blow out one candle. My daughter can be as compassionate as she is bossy. She made sure no one stayed long.

Paula and Lynn cleaned up. I had to sit on the couch and watch. The day had been stressful and I wanted to have energy left to spend my first night home with Lynn.

Paula grabbed her coat and hugged me. "Happy Birthday, Mom."

"Thank you for everything," I said. "I don't know how you manage."

She held my gaze. "We have each other. You're my role model. You never give up."

"The roles might be reversed now," I said.

She gave me a quizzical look, tossed a quick glance toward Lynn, then left without another word. Lynn stood beside me and caressed my cheek. I absorbed the sweet sensations of her slow strokes along my neck. Then she helped me up and we made our way to the bedroom.

This was it. My heart beat wildly. The pounding seemed loud enough to be audible throughout the apartment. Lynn helped me unbutton my blouse. I opened one button and she opened two. Our undressing was a seductive overture. We slid naked under the covers. I reached for her. Her body had a refreshing coolness. With no potential interruptions and constraints gone, we snuggled under the covers. When her knee slid between my legs, I froze so as not to scare her. My hand slid down her back to grab hold of her bottom. She nibbled my neck. I caught the hint of apple in her soft hair. I breathed deeper. We kissed.

This was the sign I had been waiting for. She wanted me as much as I wanted her.


I AWOKE TO the smell of bacon and Lynn leaning over me. "Good morning."

"What time is it?" I asked.

A hospital habit, where time mattered. She kissed me, assuring me that last night was not a dream.

"Seven."

"I smell bacon."

"Breakfast is almost ready. I'll set the table while you get ready. Call me if you need help." She bounced from the room without a shred of shame despite her prim catholic upbringing.

I wanted to spring up after her and twirl her around and around. My spirit was soaring. In the last few hours, the past two months of mental and emotional confusion was replaced with knowingness. There was comfort and joy in that.

Now the paradox was spirit versus body. I managed to pull myself up but it was difficult. Sleep had not replenished me. There was an overall body ache much like I experienced after a seizure. Unlike a seizure, last night's activities were to be treasured and, I hoped, repeated again and again. Lynn's glow spoke to that possibility.

Where had I found the energy last night? This morning I struggled to shower, dress, and get made up for the day.

Paula stopped on her way to work. She looked into Ben's room as she passed, and I realized that Lynn's suitcase was not there.

"How did it go?" she asked Lynn.

"Fine," Lynn answered, coming from the kitchen with a dish towel still in her hands.

"How are you, Mom?"

"Good."

"Get any sleep, Lynn?" she tossed over her shoulder as she bent to hug me.

"Yes," Lynn said, looking at me, a blush rising on her neck and face.

"Did you use Ben's room?"

"No," I answered, trying to intercept her interrogation. "We thought it better to be a bit closer the first night."

I motioned to the rocking chair in the corner. Paula was astute. We had been naïve. My bed was yet unmade and a mess. There was no extra blanket or pillow in sight. I suspected we hadn't fooled her. Ordinarily I didn't keep secrets from my daughter, but this could be explosive and I wasn't ready for the potential upheaval.

Paula slowly made her way to the front door, put her hand on the handle, and threw a look at us. "Will I see you both at the office?" Before we could respond she closed the door.

The blush on Lynn's face and neck was still apparent.

"Are you all right?" I asked.

"I wasn't ready for that."

"Neither was I."

"Do you suppose she . . . ?"

"I don't know."

Lynn twisted the dishtowel and pulled it like taffy. I moved to her. I took the towel and placed her hands on my waist. Her eyes met mine.

"Are you OK about last night?" I asked.

"Being with you is wonderful, but . . ."

"But what?" I asked, scared of what dreadful cliché she might offer.

"But I wasn't ready for Paula." She leaned her head against my chest.

"Hey, it'll be OK."

We put Lynn's things in Ben's old bedroom. Messing up both beds was not a problem. Harder to control was the eye contact, the pleasure at seeing one another, and the desire to touch. It was daring, dangerous, and exciting.

# CHAPTER FOURTEEN

TO WILLIAM, NO project but his own was worthy of development. It was up to me to keep him focused on the current design projects and meet deadlines. His habit of stopping in my office each morning with a cup of coffee resumed when I was at work. I tolerated his visits as it facilitated my watch over him.

This particular morning he waved a newspaper at me. "Barbara Streisand has started a boycott against Colorado. She must be a lesbian."

Shocked into silence, I gaped at him like a baby bird waiting to be fed. "What makes you say that?"

He tossed the paper on my desk. I read the headline:

## STREISAND ENDS CONFUSION, ENDORSES COLORADO BOYCOTT

I quickly scanned the article and saw that she had given permission to The Gay and Lesbian Alliance Against Defamation/ LA to use her name as one of the celebrities endorsing the boycott against Colorado's Amendment 2, an anti-gay initiative.

He lowered his glasses onto the bridge of his nose and frowned at me. "I don't get it. Men with men, women with women. Damn disgusting, these queers."

"Is this relevant to something, William?" I managed to say.

He had been relentless in his approaches to try to be together again. Had his ego interpreted my resistance to him as a dislike of all men? Had he seen something between Lynn and me?

"This had better not affect the deal we have on the table," William said.

We were close to securing a multi-million dollar contract that would keep the company afloat. My mind was reeling. Oh, my God. Did he suspect? Where was he going with this?

I hesitated. "How could this boycott have an effect on us?"

"We need this contract; we can't afford any bloody buggers diverting monies from business in Colorado."

Had William just threatened me? "I still don't see how gay and lesbian rights would have any bearing."

He noticed a file on my desk and picked it up. He began to read it. I didn't stop him. I wanted to avoid any further lesbian inquiries and knew he would be distracted.

"This new product you're considering is a terrible design," he said. "I'll redesign it."

"William, they're not asking for a design change, just manufacturing costs."

William would like to redesign everything. It was his talent and he was paid well for it.

"I know, but it needs to be changed," he said.

"When they ask for engineering suggestions, I'll bring it to you. Right now you have other projects that need attention."

"I'm telling you it's a bloody bad design. You would be dumb to get us involved."

I curbed my anger. "I'm only considering it. My focus is to close the new deal."

He dropped the file back on my desk. "Will you consider coming home for Christmas? No harm in that. One last Christmas."

Was this his real agenda? I still couldn't tell if his lesbian insinuations had been a threat. My intention to divorce him was also affected by the pending deal. I didn't want to expose another potential weakness in our upper management team. My health was already a vulnerability. I was not going to risk another of his adversarial moves before I closed the contract.

"Perhaps we can do that." I felt as though I had been ambushed.

"Great, I'll do the cooking. You don't have to worry about a thing." Satisfied, he left my office.


THE FINAL MEETING to close our multi-million dollar contract was set. The client, represented by the vice president of sales, the senior purchaser, and their attorney would audit the company facility to assure that it had not changed since their last inspection. A last minute assessment of management personnel, mainly me, was in order. They also wanted to examine the paperwork on our recently secured financial backing. If all was deemed acceptable, a long-term contract, with high volumes and good profit margins for Pioneering, would be finalized.

The night before the meeting it was quiet at the apartment, except for a dog whining in the distance. The pressure was on and I needed a good night's sleep. The two hardly went well together. I was allergic to sleeping pills so they were not an option.

"Do you need to review any of the paperwork?" Lynn asked me for the fifth time.

"Lynn, stop! Everything is done. I just need calm."

"Sure. Music, TV, a movie?"

"I guess mind-numbing TV." We slouched together on the sofa, covered with a blanket. I slept off and on. Mostly I listened to Lynn's soft snores and yearned for such deep sleep.

In the morning Lynn made coffee and helped me get ready. One look in the mirror made me check the quantity of cover up remaining in the makeup jar. Someone far more experienced than I was needed to cover the dark quarter moons under my eyes and general sagging throughout my face. Any other day I'd have stayed home.

As I finished dressing, I was trembling, due either to my physical affliction or stress. Taking a deep breath, I left with Lynn.

When we arrived at the office Paula took my arm. "Didn't you get any sleep?" She glared at Lynn who hurriedly went toward her office.

"It was more like little naps," I said.

We moved along the hallway to my office. I caught the sugary fragrance from the fresh pastries she had set out as we passed the conference room.

"That smells good," I said.

"Everything is ready," she said.

When we reached my office, I sat down at my desk. "You'll have to do the tour."

"Can I get you anything?" Paula asked.

"Nothing. I need to rest."

"I'll come for you after the tour then."

"Thanks. That's good."

After she left, my head dropped. I could feel the physical toll that preparing for this had taken, but I still had to convince three people that Pioneering was capable of fulfilling their contract.

It would be best if I could walk in unassisted, but I was having tremors so I sat in the wheelchair to conserve my energy. Checking a rising tear, I arranged my skirt and jacket for the most professional appearance I could present in a wheelchair. I whispered my mantra, in the hopes that it would help me hold it together. "Regulate, balance and pace." Then I told myself, "I can do this."

The door opened. Paula came in and saw that I was in the wheelchair. Her eyes met mine. "Ready?"

"Yes."

"Want me to push?"

"Please."

She held the handles, pushed me to the conference room, and whispered in my ear, "You can do it, Mom."

Coffee cups and plates with partially eaten pastries were scattered on the table. The three executives began to rise as I rolled in.

"Please don't get up," I said as Paula moved a chair from the end of the table and I positioned myself. "Let's stay comfortable."

Paula placed a folder on the table in front of me. "Does anyone need anything before I go?" After negative responses from our guests she glanced at me.

"Thank you," I said. "We'll be fine."

She exited the room.

"Thank you all for coming," I said to my clients. "It's good to see you again. Did your tour go well?"

Their replies were positive. "You have a wonderful staff. The facility is spacious, meticulous and well organized. We are very pleased."

The mental notes to breathe slowly and steadily went through my mind as I opened the folder. My hands were shaking. I pulled out three copies of the credit agreement with the bank and passed them to my right. "I believe this was the last item you requested. Please feel free to review it."

"This document satisfies our concerns on your financial backing," the attorney said after a few minutes. "We're impressed. You have met all of our demands thus far. But . . ." He paused.

My mind flicked through the possible deal breakers: my trembling, the wheelchair, what more could I do?

"How long before you can be in production?"

I controlled my impulse to moan with relief. "The equipment and materials necessary have a six-week lead time. We will supply the documentation, which will require your written approval. With your cooperation we could begin production in six weeks. The first articles would be ready for your examination seven weeks from today."

The three of them looked at each other.

"Does that work?"

"That is perfect."

The attorney pulled out two copies of the contract and handed them to me. I sat as still as a bobcat stalking its prey.

At least I hoped that was how I appeared. Inside, neurons fired with painful pricking. My temples were tight and there was a constant pressure from my eyes to my ears. I looked through the paperwork to be sure that initials were on every page. The print was becoming fuzzy.

I turned to the signature page, I added my signature to theirs and passed it back. "Thank you so much. We look forward to working with you."

The attorney slid the contract into his briefcase. He pulled out a sealed envelope, turned to me, and smiled. "Here is the check for the down payment, as per the agreement."

As they left the room, I still felt so small even though I had managed this monumental accomplishment. Confinement to a wheelchair carried a stigma I had not overcome. People either stared at me because I was odd or ignored me rather than be rude.

Lynn appeared. "Are you OK? Did they sign?"

Paula came in, looking at me expectantly.

"It's a deal," I said. "Our contract and deposit is on the table. We all still have a job."

# CHAPTER FIFTEEN

PAULA TOOK ME to my third weekly appointment with Dr. Waterford. Like a private investigator, I coaxed information from my daughter as she drove.

"How are you feeling? Are you getting enough rest? How are the dogs? What did the doctor say about the baby's growth and your health?"

"I'm seriously considering marrying Jamie," Paula said.

"Oh." I paused, surprised. "Do you love him?"

"Mom, he's kind, he works hard, and he really tries to make me happy."

"But do you love him?"

"I love a lot of the things he does. Life is easier with him around. How do I know if that's love? Did you love Dad? Did you love William? What does it all mean, anyway?"

"Well," I said carefully, "I did love them. Loving each other may not make a marriage last forever, but I believe it's a necessary component. Otherwise it's a convenient partnership. You need both to weather the storms that life will bring."

She didn't have another question with regard to love. I was relieved since I was grappling with the same dilemma, only mine seemed more complicated. Now my desire was directed toward a woman and an employee. I certainly had storms brewing.

I tuned back to Paula as she continued to answer my questions. "The vitamins still make me feel sick, but the doctor said the baby and I are growing nicely."

"I wish I could go with you to your appointments," I said.

"It's OK, Mom. I don't want you to have to go to another doctor appointment."

Paula thrived when she was taking care of someone—me, her animals, soon her baby, possibly a husband, and her brother. She occasionally had humorous updates on Ben that I enjoyed. My communication with him was sporadic at best. I was grateful for her devotion.

She parked and as we went to Dr. Waterford's office I said, "If you decide to marry him, he'll be one lucky man."

Paula and I usually hugged at my insistence. Today she gave me a warm hug. "Thanks, Mom."

Dr. Waterford started this week's appointment by saying, "Diana, I'm pleased with your progress."

"How can you say that?" I countered. "My condition is still unpredictable and without a diagnosis!"

"You haven't had any medical emergencies in the last few weeks. We can eliminate full-time care."

"Even at night?" Paula asked.

"I don't see why you can't have more privacy and control over your life," he said.

"Hey, Mom, good news!" Paula said.

She and Dr. Waterford looked at me expectantly.

Lynn would no longer have a medical reason for staying by my side at night. How would this affect us? How could I tell him that sleeping with Lynn was better medicine than any of his prescriptions? For a brief moment I wondered what he would think if I asked him to reinstate my nighttime care, but I couldn't be that transparent or appear that helpless.

"If you think I'm ready," I said, hesitant.

"I'll recommend a phone call before bed and in the morning if that relieves any anxiety," Dr. Waterford said.

"We'll see to it," Paula said.

"Diana, is there anything else you need?" Dr. Waterford asked in his appointment-concluded voice.

"Other than a diagnosis?" Then I hurriedly went on so as not to sound rude. "I'm certain if I added any more sessions or appointments, my daughter would collapse."

LYNN DID NOT try to find a way to justify to Dick her overnight stays with me. She returned home but told him that Dr. Waterford advised a nighttime phone call. We spoke to each other late at night. I was alone in the apartment. I kept the TV on for the sound of voices. I tried to make myself believe that the phone calls soothed my loneliness, but the lack of our physical intimacy left me aching.

Once again I was plunged into depression about our relationship. How long was I willing to share her with her husband? I was the one sitting alone. Lynn was with Dick and her boys. Every second she was with him was a second less that we had together. Anger welled up. Lynn's passion for me was less? Was there any chance of a harmonious, compassionate, and healthy relationship with Lynn? I had to know. I needed more. Was I being too greedy? I wanted to be loved as deeply as I loved. Could I be content with a friendship and working relationship? Was that necessary professionally but detrimental for me personally? Because of my health was it unfair of me to make such demands? My marriage to William was still an unresolved issue. I needed to be patient. But patience was not a virtue to me. It was an obstacle to achievement.

My depression began slowly then gathered momentum and sped up until I was submerged in despair. I forced myself to get up, get dressed, and be ready for work when Paula arrived to drive me to the office.

"Morning," Paula said as she and her baby bump came through the door. She opened the curtains, taking in the blanket in a bunch on the couch, soda cans on the coffee table, and the sink full of dirty dishes. "Not like you, Mom."

I tried to select the perfect words. "I'm trying to adjust to being alone."

"Look at this place. It's a mess. No plants, goldfish, or bird. It's gloomy. That therapist isn't helping."

"Give me time."

"Call Dr. Waterford and get a referral for another therapist."

"No."

"It's one of his conditions for you to live on your own."

"You wouldn't."

"Of course I would, you're scaring me."

"OK, OK. I'll look into some other therapist."

"Do you want my help?"

"No, I'll find someone."

"Mom?" she said, disbelief apparent in her tone.

"I will. I promise."

"Let me know and I'll drive you."

"OK, if need be," I said, steering her toward the door.

In the car, embarrassed that Paula had seen through me, I hid my face in Parker's fur. I panicked, knowing she wouldn't let this drop. Maybe if I got a goldfish she would back off? Who could I see? Where should I start? I could wallpaper the walls with my issues. My real issue was too terrifying to say out loud.

I took Parker with me into my office and closed the door. I flipped aimlessly through the yellow pages. The alphabetical categories offered nothing to someone who didn't know what she was looking for. After some minutes of fanning through pages, I threw the book. When it was a business need, references were easily found. Certainly I could attack this in a similar fashion. I picked up the phone book and this time looked under G. There was an actual Gay and Lesbian Community Center listed. I wrote the number and address on a yellow lined pad. I sat back, contemplating my notations.

It took several minutes for my hand to pick up the phone and make the call. The voice that answered was matter-of-fact. "Gay and Lesbian Community Center, may I help you?"

"I don't know. What is the Center about?"

"We serve the gay and lesbian community with books, a diverse resource guide, support groups, and some counseling."

"What if I'm not sure I'm gay?"

"Would you like to see a counselor?

He was soft spoken. I felt drawn. "I'd like that."

"How's tomorrow at noon with Richard?"

"That will be fine. Thank you."

Pleased with myself for having made the call, I snapped my fingers to play with Parker, who instantly jumped. I rolled a tennis ball for her to fetch.

Would Lynn go with me? Did I want her to come? I'd ask her. If she agreed, great. If not, I'd take a taxi. I rolled the ball again and said to Parker, "I wish people were as uncomplicated to deal with as dogs."

Suddenly there was a knock on the door.

"Come in."

Lynn came into my office.

"Please close the door," I said.

She did and looked at me expectantly.

"I've made an appointment to see a counselor at the Gay and Lesbian Community Center. I'd like you to go with me."

"You what? Are you serious? Why would we go there?"

"I want to find out why I feel the way I do about you." As I spoke the words the pressure in my chest lifted and my twisted gut eased. "I want to know if this is just a reaction to my sudden illness or is it more. Don't you want to know?"

"I love you," she whispered. "What more do we need to know?"

"I love you, too, but right now my life is pure chaos."

"Why?"

"I'm hoping to find out. That's why I need to know if you will go with me tomorrow."

"Well, I can drive you."

"I can call a cab if I just need a ride."

"No, I'll go."

"Good."

Lynn arrived the next day, bringing me a strong, hot coffee. We got into her car and drove to the Center, housed in a dilapidated building.

"Are you sure?" she asked one more time before parking.

"Yes," I said, determined but rattled by the building and the loitering street people. We were a long way from the sophisticated, hygienic suburban office and homes we were accustomed to.

I insisted that Lynn park close to the entrance so I could manage with just a cane. The glass door was painted with "The Gay and Lesbian Community Center" in bold black letters. Remnants of graffiti and a spider web of duct tape covered the cracks from a blow to the glass. It was backed with a sheet of plywood.

Lynn looked at me as we got to the door. As I reached for the handle, she took a breath and said, "I'll get it."

The hallway was narrow, the walls the color of scorched cream. She offered her arm and I took her hand, but she shook it off.

A male receptionist warily watched our approach from behind the desk. "Hello, can I help you?"

"I'm Diana. We have an appointment with Richard."

He checked his book and stood. "Yes, I'll let him know you're here."

We watched him walk a short distance down the threadbare carpeted hallway, where he knocked on a door. His head disappeared for a moment, then he returned to us.

"Please have a seat and Richard will be with you in a moment." He indicated a sitting area with a couch, the stuffing seeping out of the cracks and cigarette burn holes in the faded orange fabric. I took Lynn's arm and she didn't shrug me off as we chose to sit in scarred wooden chairs.

Was this the level of life I was pursuing? What if someone saw us? What if someone threw a brick or bombed the place while we were here? Were we targets now? Lynn sat upright with her muscles so tense that her trembling caused the chair to squeak.

In walked a dignified man, kindness reflected in his eyes. He greeted us warmly, hand outstretched. "Hello, I'm Richard."

I took his hand. "Hello, I'm Diana and this is Lynn."

I looked at her and saw that she was paralyzed. I nudged her and she held out her hand.

Richard gently took it. "A pleasure to meet you, Lynn."

He turned to me. "Shall we go to my office?"

I nodded and pulled Lynn along.

We entered an office filled with dated furniture. However, as Richard spoke the importance of the furnishings diminished.

"Let me explain the organization and what it can do for you. The Center is heavily dependent upon volunteers who are gay or lesbian themselves or sympathetic to our cause. They have had some basic training in crisis counseling. We lend an ear and then guide people in the direction of trained professionals if they so choose. We have a small library that you are welcome to use. We operate on the honor system; you can either read here or take books home. The limited funding we have is used to help people. As you can see we don't spend precious funds on our surroundings. We do not do long-term therapy, but we have support groups and offer a great referral service. Now what questions can I address?"

I glanced at Lynn, who was pale with no external signs of breathing. I charged ahead. "Well, I'm new to this. I don't understand what has happened to me. I've never been attracted to a woman before Lynn. Am I weird?"

"No more than billions of other people."

"You're not saying everyone is gay?" I said.

"Oh, heavens no," he said, "but we're all weird in one way or another. Here we recognize and embrace those differences."

"I've been married twice and have two children. I've never felt such a force, but I don't know if it's just Lynn or if I could be drawn to other women. And why now?"

"Sexual preference is not the total definition of a person, and is a very personal and private choice."

"Could it just be her?" I asked, glancing again at Lynn who surprisingly had not yet fainted. I took her hand, trying to break the trance.

"I'm not the person who can make the definitive decision about who you choose to love. You are. Perhaps you'd be interested in talking with a counselor?

"That would be helpful," I said. "It seems I'm in a new dimension and I don't know how to act or who to talk to."

He glanced at Lynn, then asked me, "Would you like the list of therapists we recommend?

"Yes," I said.

"Male or female?"

"Female."

Richard wrote out the list. "They are all excellent and most charge on a sliding scale. You can always call the Center for additional resources. If you're interested, there are adult lesbian support groups here at eight o'clock on Wednesday nights. Here's a card with our hours." He handed me the card and the list.

I stood up and pulled Lynn to her feet. "Thank you."

"Perhaps your friend needs some air or a drink," Richard said.

"I may need the drink!" I said.

He smiled. "There's a water fountain in the hallway."

I laughed. "Yes, well, to come here was my idea. She has religious issues."

Lynn gave me a horrified look but remained mute.

"When we begin to question our sexuality it can be a very traumatic process," Richard said. "God, however, did make all of us. It's important we be true to our inner selves. Fighting against one's nature can be a truly disastrous and painful choice. How open or out we choose to be is also a personal decision. Some find it easier to stay in the closet, their sexual preference masked from their religious communities, families, and jobs."

He had such clear explanations for the torrent of questions and thoughts I had anguished over for months.

"Thank you again. You've been very helpful."

"That's what we try to do here."

Lynn and I walked to the car, where she quickly unlocked the passenger door and opened it for me. She looked over the car as she walked hastily to the driver's side. She sat down hard in the seat, locked the doors, and stared ahead.

"I can't believe you did that to me," she said in a strained voice that escalated into shouting. "How could you? I'm not like that. I've told you it's you. Just you. He's just a sick fag. I despise those people. Air? Yes, I needed air. That was awful. I need a drink but I sure as heck wouldn't drink from their water fountain. Who knows what you'd get. That place was disgusting. Let's find a bar. Want a drink?"

"Not for me. Drugs, you know. But I'm fine stopping with you." I would rather have gone home and started arrangements for counseling. I looked at the names Richard had given me.

Lynn started to drive and continued her tirade as though she didn't hear me. "I can't stop shaking. The window, did you see it? We could have been shot? What if someone saw us?"

"We're fine. We did it, Lynn. You and I together, we took the first step."

Lynn's right brow lifted and wrinkles angled across her forehead. She pulled to a stop. The bar she had chosen was in a better part of town. It was happy hour and after chugging down the first glass of wine, she turned to me. "That, Diana, was the first step to nowhere." She turned back to the second glass and took one sip, rapidly followed by a bigger swig. "We're fine. We don't need counseling. We have each other. We don't need to associate with the likes of them."

"Maybe I do," I said.

"Whatever for?"

"I need to know more about myself, about who I am."

"Oh, Diana, you scare me. So we love each other. There's no reason to label it. Just enjoy it."

"I have to follow through with this. Pandora's box has been opened. I can't slam it closed and be content. This is my chance to discover who I really am."

"If you want to go through with this, you need to do it without me. I'll support you, I'll even drive you if it's in a decent neighborhood. But I can't participate. I hate those people. I am not like that. It's you I love."

# CHAPTER SIXTEEN

I MADE AN appointment with Anne Tiener, the fourth person on Richard's list. She had a Master's degree in Psychology; most of her clients were, as she said, practicing alternative life styles; and she was a lesbian happily involved in a committed relationship of five years.

Next morning I was showered, dressed, hair and face done and ready to go to the office. When I saw Paula approach through the front window I opened the door.

"You look good," she said.

"Thanks, I feel good. You look healthy."

"I'm growing bigger daily and the doctor said all is well."

"I worry that I'm straining your endurance."

"Mom, when I see you like this everything is worth it."

"I've made an appointment to see another therapist."

"Super. When? I'll give you a ride."

"I think Lynn's going to take me. I'll let you know if that changes." Paula looked me up and down but remained silent. We left for work.

I wrestled with Lynn's attitude. She had never expressed disgust with such vehemence. With her willingness to have a physical relationship with me, why would she be so extremely judgmental about homosexuality? She had been patient with me and my health. I would be compassionate with her. Together we would overcome this conflict.

Countless discussions later, Lynn agreed to accompany me for the first appointment with Ms. Tiener. Another seizure the evening before had left me more tired and less secure walking, but I refused to reschedule. We sat together in the well-decorated waiting room.

Mauve blinds softened the light from the bank of windows. A Queen Anne table held a pot of hot water, mugs, herbal teas, hot chocolate, and spiced cider. Burgundy upholstered chairs were arranged in a circle around the coffee table that had several issues of *Ms. Magazine* displayed.

The door opened. Two women emerged who were so intently looking at each other that they walked passed us unaware of our presence. A tall woman with stylish, slightly gray hair appeared in the doorway.

She looked at me. "Diana?"

I stood. "Yes, and this is Lynn."

Lynn rose from her chair. "Hello."

"Welcome. I'm Ms. Tiener. Have you had something to drink?"

"No, thank you," I said.

Lynn shook her head.

"If you're ready then please come in."

The waiting room colors of mauve, burgundy, and cream carried into her office. Several candles flickered. There was a hint of peppermint from her tea but no trace of perfume.

She gestured to two chairs while she sat in another, pulling gently on her black skirt to cover her crossed knees. She wore a matching blazer with a light blue button-down shirt underneath.

She directed her question to Lynn. "Let's begin. How can I be of assistance?"

Lynn blushed and turned toward me as if pleading for help. This time I refused to come to her aid. She turned back to Ms. Tiener. "I'm sorry. I'm not really prepared. This is for Diana."

"Are you a couple?" Ms. Tiener asked Lynn.

"Well, kind of, but not really."

"This is one of the issues," I said. "We're both married."

"To each other?" Ms. Tiener asked.

"No!" Lynn exclaimed.

"I'm separated. I'm trying to understand if I'm a lesbian." It occurred to me that this was my first spoken admission.

"I admit I love Diana, but it's just her," Lynn said. "It's not all women I'm attracted to. I mean, you're a beautiful woman. No, that's not how I meant it. What I mean is, I can appreciate a beautiful woman, but it doesn't mean I'm attracted to all women." She turned pink. The veins in her neck pulsed.

"I see many people who have difficulty admitting their sexual preference when they are considered abnormal by most people," Ms. Tiener politely said. "However, if you have such longings, you have them."

"But it's not normal," Lynn blurted. "The Bible says it's wrong."

"Is that what you believe, or is that what you've been taught?"

"It's what I believe."

"So you believe the loving feelings you have for Diana are wrong?"

"Well, no."

"Then perhaps it's not actually what you believe." Ms. Tiener turned to me. "Is this a difficult choice for you, Diana?"

"Well, yes. Lynn's the first woman I've wanted as a lover. I've been married to two men all my adult life. I don't know if I've changed or if it's just Lynn. I don't know what to do. I want a relationship with Lynn, but my health, my business, our situation, our husbands. It's all such a mess."

"It can be sorted out, one thing at a time. It seems to me that the first decision is whether you want my services for couples counseling or if you would prefer individual sessions."

"You can't do both?" I asked.

"No. It's a matter of ethics. If you wish to do both simultaneously that's fine. I can work with you in whichever capacity you choose and make a referral for the other."

It was grueling getting Lynn here, but it was clear she liked Ms. Tiener. This might be the only way she'd agree to couples counseling, and it might be an opportunity to become a couple in all aspects. In my physical condition could I realistically ask someone for a total commitment? Would it be better for me to focus on my personal struggles?

Ms. Tiener noted our silence. "You can take some time to decide. Would you like another appointment?"

"Yes, would Monday work?" I answered.

Checking her calendar, she gave me a choice of two times. She then wrote the date and time we agreed to on her business card and placed it in my hand. "You can leave a message if need be. I pick up all messages personally. I'll see one or both of you on Monday."

Our first session was over.

We sat in silence as Lynn drove. She stopped at a gas station where I bought her a single red rose. It embarrassed her so much she couldn't enjoy it.

"Ms. Tiener is wonderful, don't you think?" Lynn said as we neared the office.

"Does that mean you'll go with me on Monday?"

"I don't know. I have to ask Dick."

"You're OK with asking your husband if you can go to couples counseling with me?" I asked totally mystified.

"Well, he is my husband and we've been together for a long time."

"How much longer do you expect to be together?"

"Forever, I suspect. But he's OK with us."

"He's OK with our friendship, our intimacy, or our living together?"

"He likes you. He'd like to be an integral part of the relationship."

"What does that mean?"

"I know you're not real keen on him, but he cares about you."

My head was throbbing. "Is it OK with him if you move out and live with me full time?"

"Diana, I can't do that."

"Why not?"

"I don't know. I'm scared."

"Are you afraid I'm going to stay an invalid or die on you and you'll be left alone?"

"No. Well, maybe. That's part of it. I don't know."

"If that's the problem, I can understand. We can give it time and see what happens," I said. "But if I get better? What then?"

"Diana, I don't know."

"Lynn, I want you every day and every night, not just now and then."

"Me, too, Diana. I really do."

I was exhausted when we got to my apartment. "I'll have Paula take me to my appointment."

"I didn't say that I'm not going."

"And you haven't said that you are. My life will not be controlled by your husband."

I GRABBED FRESH bedclothes from my dresser. There was a thud as my 38 special hit the drawer bottom. I'd forgotten it was there. Dropping the nightgown, I picked up the gun. It was cool in my hand, well-balanced and weighty for its size. It gave me a sense of power. I held it for several moments. I opened the chamber to see the butt end of each bullet. I closed the chamber and released the safety and touched the trigger. I could end the pain, the questions, the waiting for the next sick twist in my life. Tempting as it was, I took my finger from the trigger and reset the safety. I placed it back in my drawer, hidden among my clothes.

In bed, Lynn's words rolled like a tumbleweed through my mind. She wants me, maybe, under certain circumstances and if her husband approves. I had invited her to join me on a complicated and intimate journey. Did she change the direction? Was I being asked to allow her husband to join in our relationship?

Getting up, I took the gun from the drawer, and slipped it under my pillow. I wanted the sense of power next to my body.

# CHAPTER SEVENTEEN

"DIANA," MS. TIENER said as she took in the otherwise empty waiting room, "do come in."

Paula had dropped me off and would return in an hour. Arms pushing hard on the big rubber wheels, I rolled into her office. A journal with a blue dragonfly on the cover and pen lay in my lap. I was here to learn. It was back to school.

"Where would you like to start today?" Ms. Tiener began.

"I think it would be wise to tell you about my health."

"Fine."

"To date I am not diagnosed although I've had a battery of tests. My symptoms mimic MS but that was proven negative. My capabilities range from walking with a cane to as you see me now, only strong enough to wheel myself around in this thing." I banged my hand on the handle, an exclamation mark of disgust. "I have brain lesions, constant fatigue, allergic reactions to a multitude of medications, and occasionally seizures. I'm under enormous pressure at work. I am separated from my second husband, who is also employed by my company. He has been trying to oust me as the CEO by manipulating the board of directors. He has possibly threatened my newfound sexuality and attraction to Lynn. Of that I'm not certain, but he is an alcoholic narcissist and I don't trust him." I had been concentrating on a candle that Ms. Tiener had lit on the table between us. I looked up and noted that she was writing on a tablet. She caught my look and the warmth in her gaze helped me to go on. "Lynn was with me when my body first began to fail. We were on a camping trip. It was my hope that the wilderness and the solitude would help us come to an understanding of what was happening between us. However, what it did was bring me to the brink of my will to live."

Ms. Tiener regarded me for a moment. "The things you have shared are life-altering events. Each one can be incredibly stressful. I see that you brought a notebook. Let's prioritize, perhaps make a list. Do you agree?"

I nodded. I like to make lists. Unfortunately, I can't delegate this list. I picked up my pen and opened my notebook.

"What did you mean when you said, 'to the brink of my will to live'?" Ms. Tiener asked without preamble.

"Ah, well," I stammered, "I've begun to sleep with my revolver under my pillow. It gives me a sense of power. When I became ill I lost so much control over my life. The only thing that is completely in my power is my decision to live or die."

"As I said, you have been through more in the last few months than most people deal with in a lifetime," she said gently but with an edge of firmness. "I'm here to help you regain a sense of self. You need to be patient."

I responded with my own version of firm determination. "I don't consider patience a virtue. To me it's a hindrance, a false promise like hope, peddled to people so they will accept their lives as is. My health issues have taught me that we have no control over our destiny, no matter how hard we fight." I glared at Ms. Tiener, waiting for her to give me some empty counselor rhetoric. I ran my moist hands firmly along my thighs to stop the trembling that began in the pit of my stomach, then ran to my neck and down my arms. A desperate plea to my body not to go into a seizure.

Ms. Tiener watched me closely. "What is going on right now, Diana?"

"I don't want to lose control of my body."

"It's OK," she said. "This is where you can be vulnerable, and no one is going to hurt you."

I flashed back to the school nurse letting me smash the pretty teacup on the floor. She had told me that it wasn't important, I was. With tears flowing I began my story again with Ms. Tiener.

This time I started with the sexual, physical, and emotional abuse that my stepfather and mother inflicted on me and all my siblings. I told her my mother had to take me to the doctor regularly to deal with yeast infections. She told the doctor they were from the toilet seat. Why did he believe her? I told her that the school nurse had wanted to call my mother after I revealed that my stepfather said it was his job to teach me about sex. The nurse wanted to call the sheriff, too, but I pleaded with her not to. What if no one believed me? What if my brother and sisters didn't back me up? It would all be so much worse. I was afraid I would lose my family. My mother.

We came to the end of our time. Ms. Tiener had pulled another box of tissues from a cupboard and handed it to me. "Diana, you have enormous strength and courage. It's not your nature to give up. Ever."

We settled on two sessions a week after Ms. Tiener extracted a promise from me. "One more thing, Diana. You will not attempt to take your life."

"I promise." I said with a force of spirit that I had not felt in a long time.

"Good, 'til Thursday then."

"Thursday." I agreed, "and thank you."


AFTER MY SESSIONS with Ms. Tiener I spent time writing a more legible and complete synopsis of my hurried scribbles. I added thoughts or plans that arose from my insights.

I told Lynn that for now I wanted my own counseling sessions. I'm sure she was relieved, but she wanted to know everything that went on. I never let her read my notes from beneath the dragonfly. I think she had Ms. Tiener under her skin. She tried hard not to let it show but she couldn't help asking about her and commenting on how different she was from other lesbians. I wondered how large her sampling of lesbians was. Two, I suspected. With Lynn not being one, that left me and Ms. Tiener.

Lynn and I were having dinner, just the two of us, at my

apartment. I decided to put my cards on the table. "I'm not well, Lynn. I could die soon."

"Oh, don't say that."

"It's true. But I'm not dead yet and I'm going to get on with whatever life I have. Parker and I need a real home." I rushed on before she could derail me. "I want a small farm. I want to raise cattle, exotic animals, rabbits, or whatever, and create another income stream from animal husbandry. I can't do it all by myself. I'd like for us to do this together. What do you think?"

"I think it would be fun. You're so good at making money, I'm sure it would be a good investment." She raised my hand to her lips and brushed it with kisses. Sparks raced up my arm, straight to my heart.

I hugged her and pulled her into my lap. "I'm going to start checking into it with a realtor after Christmas. Are you OK with that?"

"Of course."

Perhaps if we had a place, our place, she would be more comfortable, more secure about a future with me. I wanted to prove that I had a lot to offer. Still, I could feel that I was holding a part of myself back. Her love was conditional. Even now, her agreement to buy a place together was predicated on my ability to make it a good investment for her. Are my stepfather's words imbedded so deeply that I still pit myself against those who make me feel that I have to prove my worth? Food for thought, and a discussion with Ms. Tiener to be sure. Did I deserve to be loved? We had discovered in one of our sessions that the unconditional love my grandparents had shown me had likely saved me.

Christmas with William consumed an entire session with Ms. Tiener. Why had I agreed to go? Oh yes, the clever little ambush that he had maneuvered. Paula agreed after asking me why I was putting us all though William's torture. "For the last time," was how she voiced her curt response to my explanation. I had no recourse but to go through with my agreement. I hoped that he would be as amenable when I hit him with the divorce papers; but as I was learning in Ms. Tiener's office, my unflinching determination did not guarantee the desired outcome. I was attempting to cultivate patience. Ms. Tiener said it was the opposite side of the same coin as determination. You need both.

Lynn and I had the day after Christmas together. We each had spent the necessary time with our respective families. Now it was our, albeit limited turn. Knowing I could soon own a home with her temporarily pacified me.

The apartment smelled delicious from the food I had brought home from William's and the pine-scented candles. We held each other and nibbled on holiday candies and leftovers.

"How was your day?" I asked.

"It was great. The boys ate and hung out. They got new clothes and some extra cash."

"What did Dick get you?" I was uncertain that I wanted to know.

"Oh, we don't exchange gifts. There's really no point. We have what we need. Did you and William exchange gifts?"

"I gave him a tie and he was beyond generous. He's always been a good gift giver. He thinks it makes up for his bad behavior. Maybe men don't emotionally mature past twelve."

As much as I despised gifts from a manipulative ex, the thought of a relationship that didn't permit gift giving was also distasteful. I wouldn't let that happen.

"I have a little something for you," I said, getting up to retrieve the box.

"You already gave me a gift at the office."

"That was from the company. This is from me."

When I returned, she had a small black box with a red bow on her lap. "And this is from me."

We exchanged the boxes and unwrapped them. She loved the leather-bound journal. I was delighted with the Yanni and Enya tapes. "A lot has happened since I heard these last."

"An awful lot."

I didn't know if her emphasis on awful was reflective of bad awful or a huge amount of awful. I decided to move on without finding out.

"I'm going to call a realtor on Monday. What are your house specifications?"

We had a lengthy discussion listing our dream requirements, which included a fireplace, gazebo, wraparound porch, outbuildings, tall trees, a stream or lake, and a magnificent view. And with that I led her to the bedroom. After crawling into bed, we spent the rest of our time together snuggling and caressing. Merry Christmas to me. When I awoke she was gone.


MONDAY ARRIVED AND I called the realtor. Her message said she would be back on January 11th. I made a note to call then.

Lynn came to take me to lunch and then drop me off for my session with Ms. Tiener. I noted that Lynn seemed eager to see Ms. Tiener when she came out to call me into her office. They exchanged a greeting and I rolled after her.

We got settled in our usual seating arrangement.

"Is there any significance to Lynn being here?" Ms. Tiener asked.

I looked to the door.

"It's locked and she can't hear a thing."

"I think she just wanted to get another look at you." I laughed without humor.

Ms. Tiener didn't respond but waited.

"She's agreed to help me buy a house," I said.

"Is that for you to live in together?"

"I don't know. She says it is, but I'm reluctant to push. I still don't have a diagnosis and my health is tenuous."

"You may have to make hard decisions even with unstable health."

I started to cry. I hated to be pitiful but I was worn out. My tears used up her box of tissues and our time. She told me tears were a process of healing. I dried my eyes and wiped my nose.

"My daughter, Paula, helped me do the legwork on the divorce proceedings," I said, as though I was presenting a report to a teacher.

Ms. Tiener gave a slight nod and waited. I felt as though I had her approval.

"Paula was delighted."

"I'm certain the impact of your illness has had a dramatic effect on your family and your employees. Everyone benefits from your recovery. This closure with William will help."

I didn't want to feel her disapproval, but I had to tell her that William was staying on as an employee of the company. I wondered when I would no longer feel like a little girl vying for approval. From whom? My mother?

"Does allowing him to remain benefit the company?" she asked.

"I'm not sure. I have to take one step at a time with him. He's reactionary and I don't want my position challenged by the board. William has credentials that I don't have."

"You know your business, Diana," Ms. Tiener said.

I decided to share the rest of my rationale. "I've been quietly putting out feelers with other companies to ease him out. So far nothing has come of it."

"Remarkable benevolence. Keep in mind that carrying someone for too long makes their legs weak and yours crumble." Her final words echoed in my mind as I rolled out to the waiting room and saw Lynn. "Be careful not to lose yourself."

I wondered how much I would be willing to compromise to be loved.

# CHAPTER EIGHTEEN

THE PHONE RANG. It was early. Only Lynn called so early.

"Hello," I said, speaking softly.

"This is Dr. Waterford." His voice sounded like it was charged with electricity. "It's Lyme disease, Diana."

"What?"

"I just got a letter from the Center for Disease Control."

"What are you saying, Dr. Waterford? I don't understand. I thought I had a Lyme titer months ago when this nightmare first began?"

"Lyme is a poorly understood disease. The CDC has more expertise to analyze lab results. I wanted to be thorough. You've had so many symptoms. It was difficult to pinpoint a cause. Now we know what we're dealing with, and it's treatable." He went from doctor-patient-voice to medical-detective-voice. "Do you know when and where you got a tick bite? It must be somewhere outside Colorado. To date we haven't had any reported cases originating from here."

"At an air show in Oshkosh, but that was a while ago." I was trying to take this all in. Hadn't I told him about the tick bite early on, when we were so baffled by the sudden onset of bizarre symptoms?

"That's it! Wisconsin!" He sounded like he had just discovered another planet. Then he returned to his usual seriousness. "I consulted with the CDC about a treatment plan."

My mind skittered back from the infectious air show. "What can I expect? How treatable is Lyme disease? How long before I'm cured?"

"Six weeks of daily IV's with a medication called Rocephin."

"That's it? Six weeks and I'll be well?"

"That's the usual treatment plan. With the drugs that are already in your system and your sensitivity to so many, we could experience some complications."

"But ultimately it's completely curable?"

"That is our hope. We won't know until you start treatment and we see how you react."

"But I could totally recover?"

"I'm reluctant to say that. I don't know yet what effect the medication will have on the brain lesions, and if any of your impairments are a result."

"How soon can we start treatment?" I asked. Suddenly my lists were possible. I'd lost so much time.

"The IV will take about an hour each day."

I could hear him talk to someone else. He returned to the line. "Would you like to come in today, or we can arrange for a nurse to come to your home or office."

"I'm at home today."

"My office will call you shortly to set up a time today and an ongoing schedule." He paused. I waited, fearful to hear anything dreadful, but he simply said, "Diana, you will definitely be getting better."

And in his brusque manner he hung up before I could utter, "Thank you."

I fell against the bed pillows. Air expelled from my lungs. A tremor began in my chest. I began to quake all over. A giant flood of tears gushed, spilling onto the bed linens. I was a waterfall of hope, excitement, relief, and rage. I reached for my journal to write about this remarkable day, but my hands were shaking and I needed to use the bathroom. I made my way across the floor, trying to get my bearings. Doubt crept in. Had I imagined the phone call? Did I hear his words correctly? I had resigned myself to this existence until I met the terms I had made with Kathleen and Steve. I should call them. I should call Paula. I should call Lynn.

The phone rang. I picked it up, wondering whose voice I was going to hear. "Hello?"

"Is this Diana?"

"Yes," I said carefully.

"This is Nora with patient care calling on behalf of Dr. Waterford's to schedule your treatment."

"Yes! Yes! When can you come?" I pinched myself and it hurt.

"It's important to do the treatments at the same time every day and it takes about an hour. Dr. Waterford said you were home today. What time suits you?"

With my thoughts going all over the place, I'd neglected to consider a time that would work every day. Of course I wanted to start right now, but I had to think of Paula, Lynn, Ms. Tiener, work, and all manner of obligations.

"What hours are possible?" I asked.

"We're available 24 hours a day."

"Will the treatments have any side effects."

"Not usually; however, we can't be sure."

"Can someone be here by 11 a.m. today? I really want to get started."

"Will that time work seven days a week?"

"I'll make it work. During the week I'll be at my office."

"Either location is fine, as long as the time stays consistent. Do you mind holding for one moment?"

"That's fine." I'd been on hold for three months. We sorted through the logistical details and our conversation was over. It was 8 in the morning. I had three hours to wait before the rest of my life began. I called Paula at the office.

"Pioneering," she answered.

"I'm, I'm . . ."

"Mom! What's wrong?"

"Nothing, not a thing."

"Is there something wrong with your mother?" I heard Lynn ask in the background.

"Mom! What is it?"

"The nurse is coming . . ."

"Nurse? For what? I'll be right there!" Panic was rising in her voice.

"I'll go with you," Lynn was saying.

"No," I said. "Dr. Waterford called. He diagnosed me. I start treatment today."

I heard a moment of dead silence. Then a screech that made me hold the phone away from my ear. I heard Paula tell Lynn who sounded like she was laughing and crying at the same time. I wished I were there.

Paula came back on the line. "I'm coming over."

I heard Lynn say, "Me, too!"

Then they were gone. Most likely racing out the door.


I WAS SO thrilled to tell Ms. Tiener that I began talking before the door closed as we entered her office. She leaned over the arms of my wheelchair and hugged me. Then we positioned ourselves as usual.

I shared my expectations of what I could be doing very soon. She encouraged me to focus on what is realistic. "You're not well yet. And you, of all people, know the future is very precarious."

I wrote in my dragonfly journal, which was starting to have frayed pages. I wanted to capture our words; they resonated with wisdom each time I reread them. I wanted the most from what Ms. Tiener helped me to recognize and come to terms with.

Today she gave me a homework assignment, to make a list of my expectations. It was completed before the taxi pulled up to my apartment. I prioritized actions I wanted to take, trying hard to stay within my present capabilities. When I was feeling better, I hoped I would have more time to do other things.

Paula called to fill me in on the status of our current projects at Pioneering.

"Great," I said. "Enough business. You OK?"

She became silent. "Paula?"

I heard sniffling. Was she crying? My strong and brave daughter who never broke down. Was there something wrong with the baby? Was work too much? Was I?

I tried to reach her through the phone. "Sweetie, what is it?"

"Jamie brought me a dozen roses and asked me to marry him again. He won't stop, Mom. He just keeps after me."

"And that's bad?" I was relieved, trying to be sympathetic. Pregnancy can make you crazy at times.

"Roses!"

"You don't like roses?"

"He's just so nice."

"Well?" I said, after a minute.

"Well, what?"

"Are you going to marry him? What did you tell him?"

"Nothing. I just cried."

"What did he do?" I asked, starting to feel sorry for Jamie.

"He laughed and said he'd keep asking."

"Do you want him to stop asking?"

"No, I'm just tired and moody and don't want to be pushed."

"Maybe you should tell him you want to wait until after the baby is born."

"I guess I could."

"It would take the pressure off you right now."

"Thanks, Mom."

"I'm hoping that I can be less of a burden on you."

"I don't mind it. You're my mom."

"Yes, but soon your baby will need all of you."

"It's one of the reasons I don't want to commit to Jamie right now. I want to see what it's like to be a mom before I'm a wife."

"I don't think this would be so hard for you if you loved him."

"Mom, I don't want to talk about it anymore."

"I'm here if you do. I love you."

"Love you, too. Good night."

After four weeks of treatment, changes were occurring rapidly. I was feeling better. Walking no longer required a deliberate mental focus, but it was difficult to stop the habit. What if I didn't place my feet right because I took it for granted too soon? What if all the progress was suddenly zapped away again? I felt like a juggler between my still fluctuating health and the daily challenges that faced a growing company. It was hard to keep all the balls in the air and know when to let a ball drop.

Buying a home was symbolic. Once again I was taking up residence in the world. It was a major decision. I knew that. Was I mentally, physically, or emotionally ready for such a leap? I believed so. Lynn wanted to invest, more than financially, I hoped. Paula would tell me exactly what she thought of any deal I might consider. A team of three women to conquer the world.

The search team became a foursome when Lynn involved Dick. She said he had extensive knowledge assessing and buying real estate. Neither Paula nor I liked his involvement, but we dealt with it. I needed Lynn's money for the down payment. I hadn't been taking a paycheck from the company since I had hired William. The company couldn't afford to pay us both. I felt that I was in the same boat as Paula: but instead of a baby, a house was creating a bond. What kind of bond was the question still to be answered.

By the end of the fifth week of my hour-long IV treatment, the improvements were obvious to all. I was walking unassisted. I still had occasional spasms, numbness, and an ache at the temple by my left eye, but I had real hope of achieving my optimal physical health again. Conversely, fundamental parts of my psyche would never be the same.

"I'm different," I said to Ms. Tiener as we sat comfortably sipping herbal tea in her office. I noticed she had a new plant, an African violet that was starting to bud. I could just barely make out the subtle fragrance. It was fresh and bright, like Spring, which was fast approaching. "Now each day offers opportunity.

For the present, I'm in control and it feels magnificent. But I've been to the brink of helplessness and despair. I hope this personal disaster has made me more compassionate; and yet at the same time I feel even less tolerant of those without any dedication to life. It's a gift and we need to be grateful, not throw it away. Does that make sense?"

"Yes."

"It's shifted my expectations of others as well as what I expect of myself."

"Our view of life can radically alter when we are faced with our own mortality."

"I was literally stopped in my tracks," I said.

"How have your expectations of others shifted?"

"I've learned to delegate with respect."

Ms. Tiener shot me a look of confusion.

"What I mean is, I ask for what I need based on a person's abilities, then I get out of the way so they can do what they do best. But now I can tell if their heart's not in it, and I don't want to tolerate that. Why waste time? My daughter was uncompromising in her devotion to me. She never gave up."

"What about Lynn?"

I took a minute. You would think after endless hours mulling over every detail of our relationship, I would have had it figured out. Perhaps I wanted to make my sexual attraction to Lynn be more meaningful. I'd have to contemplate that little idea later. I did my best to tell Ms. Tiener how I felt.

"Lynn had respect for me when I was strong, and she came to my rescue in my need. She gives fully as an employee. Her friendship brought love and laughter, although sporadic." I brushed a tear away. Ms. Tiener slid the Kleenex box closer to me. I took a tissue. "We're looking for small acreage with a home and potential for an animal business. She's offered $50,000 as upfront money."

"Is her emotional commitment as generous as her financial commitment?"

"I'm sensing that she gets off on the competition between Dick and me for her attention. I'm hoping that my improving health and our joint purchase of a home will bring clarity to her. I don't want to screw anything up by pushing too hard."

"Lynn is a grown woman. She is making her own choices as are you. It seems to me that from what I have witnessed, you have been transparent about your wishes. You have to decide how many more compromises you want to make for her." She glanced at the clock and pushed on. "And what about William? From what you've said he hasn't been giving you his respect or his dedication for a long time."

"The divorce is finalized," I said with some pleasure.

"And his employment?" she asked shrewdly.

# CHAPTER NINETEEN

WILLIAM AGREED TO pay me half of the equity in our gentleman's ranch once it sold. We left his job at Pioneering alone; as I rightly intuited, he wasn't stupid, or maybe he paid attention to counsel from his attorney. His substantial earnings outweighed any vengeful desire to haggle over our personal assets. One step at a time. My mantra—regulate, balance, and pace—was as effective now as it was when I used it to stay acutely aware of my physical limitations.

The home search with Lynn, Dick, Paula, and I netted results. Several properties were interesting to us, but one ranch stood out. The house was fairly new with two metal barns perched on 40 acres of gently rolling hills, situated on the eastern plains of the Rockies. The commute to work would be half an hour longer than we'd initially planned, but I was finally cleared for driving and had a new appreciation for downtime, a time to reflect.

There was no time to be alone with Lynn on our first viewing of the property. As the realtor drove the four of us back to the office, our communication was restrained. I believed Lynn had to be as excited as I was. I could feel it. I knew her.

When Lynn and I were finally alone in my office, we burst out in unison, "It was perfect!"

"The whole house was full of light," I said.

"The fireplace," Lynn cut in.

"The bathrooms are huge."

"It's so spacious."

"And the outbuildings are big enough for a business."

"I want a horse," Lynn said, then added with a flirtatious grin, "We should have two so we can ride together."

"Why not?" I said. "So, it's you and me, we're partners?"

"Yes, but I need to talk with Dick."

"What! Why?" I couldn't believe what I was hearing. Dread hit me like a clenched fist in my stomach.

She must have seen my unease because she whirled around to me and grabbed my hands. "Don't worry."

"I thought it was your money and your decision."

"It'll be fine," she said. "I'll talk to him tonight."

My destiny was at stake. If Dick controls this decision, then what have I been waiting and planning for? My lease was nearly up. The divorce settlement was not yet available. I decided I could wait another night.

"WELL?" I ASKED Lynn the next morning.

"Dick's concerned about the distance. He says it's almost to Kansas, and he doesn't understand why anyone needs that much land," she said. "You're just starting to drive. What if there's a medical issue? It's a long way from any help."

"I appreciate his concern," I said wryly.

"He's got our well-being in mind."

"Yes, but we did want distance from Denver and privacy. This has everything we were looking for. For me, the driving would be a plus, not a detriment. It's just a few more miles." I felt as though I was in a tug of war with this man. An idea came to me. "Why don't I contact the realtor and tell her you and I want to drive out ourselves and look at it again? We can see the place without all the distractions."

She started to smile and I could see that she liked the idea. "Sounds good."

We were on our way in 20 minutes. I drove. Dick's fussing about my ability to drive was ludicrous.

I stopped the car at the entrance. I was excited. I noted that the pasture land was fenced on all sides with barbed wire—good cattle fencing, I thought. Slowly I drove through tall white posts that bordered the entrance to the narrow graveled driveway. The place was affecting me much like the wilderness. I knew in my heart and every fiber of my being that some way, somehow, this place would be mine.

Lynn was beaming as we stepped from the vehicle. We stood by the car for several minutes, scanning the distant mountain range that hovered on the edge of the clear skyline. The prairie grasses waved as gusts of wind swept across the vast plains. Lynn joined me on the driver's side and discreetly took my hand.

"This is beautiful," I said.

"Yes," she replied, and we walked slowly toward the house.

The owners welcomed us and graciously stayed several paces behind as we toured the house. Occasionally we would accidentally-on-purpose nudge each other to indicate our delight. I commented on the decor and furnishings, trying not to come across as too excited. We left the house to survey the rest of the property.

I could tell by Lynn's stride that she was giddy. We stood at one of the farthest corners of the property, looking at the scope of the land. Then on we went to the barns. A big red tractor was the sole resident of the first building. In the second building shelves held the remnants of a garage sale. Prices remained on the items. It felt enormous. Lynn almost toppled me over when she suddenly wrapped her arms around me in a giant bear hug, followed by a noisy smooch on my cheek.

"This is it, isn't it?" she exclaimed.

"Yes. For me, it most certainly is. What about for you?" I hugged her tighter, resting in her embrace.

She whispered "yes" in my ear.

I trembled with relief, excitement, and fatigue. My body was still in recovery and I had walked a lot. Our hug tightened and we shared a long kiss.

We chatted about our plans for this and that as we walked to the car. When we reached it, I made my collapse on the seat as unnoticeable as possible. I drove slowly, taking in the property from every angle, until it was no longer visible.

"Let's call and make an offer. It's time to close this deal."
Lynn shocked me with her bold stance.

"You've made me very happy. It's the beginning of a new
life. Together."

"You do understand that I'm doing this without Dick's
approval," she said quietly.

I understood immediately that the wedge between Lynn and
Dick had just widened. What I didn't know was if this was her
break from him in all ways. I didn't want to tarnish the moment,
so I remained silent and smiling.

She went on with her financial strategy. "I'll call my
stockbroker and sell some of my shares after they've accepted
our offer." She owned stock from a former company. With all
the spinoffs, mergers, and stock splits, Lynn was financially
comfortable through her own efforts.

After we got back to the office I called the realtor to begin
the paperwork and set up an appointment to sign documents that
afternoon.

Paula came into my office as I hung up the phone. "What's
going on, Mom? You and Lynn look like you're up to something."

I was startled. "What?"

"You both look as though you have a light bulb glowing
inside."

"We're making an offer today on that property we saw
yesterday."

"You decided," she responded without enthusiasm.

"Yes. I can't wait to have room to breathe. I'll be able to get
Parker out of your office."

"Dick's going along with this?"

"She's doing it without him," I said with a victory grin.

"I can't believe it."

"It's true." I felt so grateful at how things were unfolding that
I wanted my daughter to be as excited. "I couldn't have come
this far without you, sweetheart. You saved me from despair
many times."

"Mom, I know. We all knew."

"What do you mean?"

"Dr. Waterford cautioned all of us about the danger of your giving up."

I gazed at her as remembered secretive looks and quiet conversations flashed across my mind. "I guess I shouldn't be surprised."

"He said to watch out for unusual behavior. Like when I found you that day with your place a mess and you not showered. Why do you think I bullied you to get in touch with a therapist?"

Mental note; call Kathleen. "Now it's your turn for all the attention and care you can stand. There's my first grandchild to get ready for. And he will need a place to ride his pony."

Paula laughed. She turned to leave, then looked back. "You know, Mom, this was too hard for Ben. That's really why he left."

"I know. I'll reach out to him when I'm settled."

I called Kathleen after Paula left. We had shared a celebratory phone call when Steve told her that I was diagnosed. She had asked me to lunch, but I was trying to make up for lost time and I hadn't seen her yet. The three-month time frame on the dying-with-dignity issue had come and gone. It was time for me to relieve them of such a responsibility.

We caught up on my healing progress. She knew about the office politics from her husband. We didn't waste much time hashing over my divorce with William. He had never treated Steve with respect. They circled each other with caution. William had never liked the fact that I had gone to Steve instead of him to start Pioneering. I asked about their children and she said they were sending off for college applications.

"I'm going to be a grandma any day now," I said.

"Diana, I'm so glad the diagnosis came before the baby. You can welcome this new life with pure joy."

"Thank you for holding my secret. So much was out of my hands. To have control over my life or death made my will to keep fighting stronger."

"You gave Steve an opportunity to find his place in the world, which in turn allowed us to raise our children. It's mutual appreciation."

We ended with a promise to have lunch very soon. I wondered what she and Steve would think about Lynn and me. The fact that we were buying a residence together would not go unnoticed by people in the company.

On Monday Lynn, Paula, and I waited anxiously for the seller's response to our offer on the property. I could hardly stand the jitters from not hearing anything by late afternoon. I called the realtor. She said technically they had until the next evening to respond. That only slightly eased my mind.

We were about to leave my office when the phone rang. Paula answered and held it out to me. "It's your realtor."

I took the receiver. They watched me as I mouthed, "They accepted our offer." I heard the realtor say, "They're anxious to get it done. Can you meet at the title company next week?"

I looked at Paula. Her stomach was bulging. Her due date was this week. I told the realtor, "Perfect." I thanked her and hung up the phone.

Lynn stepped in and gave me a hug. I turned to Paula and tried to hug her, then decided it was easier to pat her belly.

"I can bring the dogs to run, they're so cooped up at my place." She picked up her purse. "I'm going home. Jamie's making dinner and I want him to rub my back." She waddled out the door.

I closed the door and turned to Lynn. We met each other's eyes. Each of us looking for our own version of what we each wanted or expected. I decided I was ready to hear how this was affecting her marriage. "You haven't told me what Dick said about this."

"He thinks I've thrown my money away; but as he said, it's my money to waste."

"Do you feel that way?"

"I think we can build a profitable business. After all, you've been ranching your whole life. Have you decided how we should start?"

"I haven't decided anything," I said. "This is a joint venture."

Lynn took my hand and kissed it. "This is so wonderful."

"Here's one thought," I said, lacing her fingers with mine. "Paula, Ben, and I raised rabbits when we lived with William. The kids sold them to the local pet stores. We could move those cages and setups to the big barn. It would allow expansion of the rabbitry if the need is there, and we could diversify."

"Sounds good," she said. "Dick could help us set it up."

My mind started to race. How much of a role did Lynn want Dick to play? He wasn't included in my vision of our love nest.

I questioned her, remembering her vague comments about his interest in me. "Dick's willing to help us even though there's nothing in it for him?"

"Sure. He'll want to give us a hand."

Perhaps I was making too much of this. But I didn't think so. We hadn't even closed yet and I already felt forced to make uncomfortable compromises. I felt like this one was necessary. "William will help too, he'll be ecstatic to get the rabbit setup off his property.

Lynn seemed to sense my unease and tried to reassure me. "I know that most importantly it will be your home." We had agreed on that from the start, but she had invested a large sum. She had rights, too.

"And you're OK with that?"

"As long as I'm welcome."

"Of course you're always welcome."

# CHAPTER TWENTY

PAULA WAS MISERABLE. She had gained a lot of weight during her pregnancy. I had a large swivel fan placed near her desk. She insisted on working and tending to Parker; she said the little dog soothed her. She refused to stay home and rest.

"Do you want me to stay with you?" I asked.

"No, Mom, I'll call when I go into labor. You've got to be with me when it happens."

"Wouldn't miss it."

Around quitting time the next day her yelp came loud and clear from down the hallway. "Mom!"

I and the 20 other people still in the building reached her simultaneously.

"Take me to the hospital," she gasped.

Escorting her to the car, I asked, "Did your water break?"

"No, but the pressure is so intense I know this is it," she said through gritted teeth.

I got her loaded into the passenger seat. Everyone sent her off with good wishes.

I drove to the hospital, trying not to let Paula see how nervous I was. Each time her hand gripping the door handle turned white, I knew she was having a contraction. She emitted little moans. I drove faster. Someone at the office must have called Jamie. He was pacing in front of the hospital doors.

The doctor assured us that everything was progressing nicely. I worried that the stress I had put on her would strain her labor and delivery. When I gave birth to Paula I couldn't dilate. The doctor back then said my muscles wouldn't relax because of the strenuous farm labor I did. They did a C-section after 28 hours. I never believed that it was the hard work. How many toiling women gave birth?

For my daughter stress was manageable. Pain was not. Two minutes in the labor room and she ordered an epidural. Delivery of a tiny, purple naked baby boy came some hours later. I was so relieved she didn't have to have a C-section. Jamie and I stayed with Paula through the night. She kept the nurses jumping for pain medication. I kept peering at this wrinkled little miracle. My first grandson hadn't a clue how fervently I had prayed to be here when he arrived in the world. I was ready to be a grandmother.

The next morning Paula and baby Nathan were released. Fussing over her and the baby was a treat for me. I had already bought baby clothes, one outfit with a baseball player and one with a cocker spaniel puppy. I was there for two days happily doting on my daughter and grandson. When I thought I should let the new family bond and have some privacy, Paula disagreed.

"Mom, don't leave. I want you here. Can you stay?"

"Of course, I just don't want to interfere."

"You're not," she said, glancing at Jamie, who nodded.

He was the picture of a proud daddy. He couldn't stop grinning and stroking Nathan. He tried to make Paula comfortable in every way he could imagine. I was extremely grateful that I was able to be there for her. She had been there for me, unflinchingly.


A FEW WEEKS after the baby was born, I had an appointment with Dr. Waterford. He was pleased with my progress. The treatment had been successful. No additional drugs were prescribed nor would more therapy be required. I would have a follow-up visit in one month.

"Recovery will be gradual and will take time. Your body is still weak. You must be patient. In some cases Lyme can reoccur. We still need to monitor you." He gave me that look, the one that makes me feel either like a little girl or a specimen. "Diana, you know that you've been given a gift."

I wasn't sure what he meant. I had nearly died, and I had suffered for over five months without knowing if I would ever recover. Then I thought about my new grandson and that the perseverance of this man had made it possible for me to be with Paula. And that trumped all else. "I'm very grateful for getting my life back. I was able to be at the birth of my first grandson."

"You also have new clarity to help you chart your future."

I was stunned. When I reached the car I wrote his philosophical statement down in my dragonfly journal. It seemed fitting. My next stop was a session with Ms. Tiener.

She greeted me with, "You're glowing today!"

"I'm a grandmother of a healthy baby boy. And Dr. Waterford just told me the Lyme treatments were a success. And we've closed on a beautiful property."

"Congratulations!" She smiled. "Such major hurdles, Diana."

I returned her smile. "Lynn and I can start moving in next weekend."

"Is she leaving her husband?"

"Not immediately, but both of our names are on the deed."

"She held true on the property acquisition. That's good."

"Lynn risked a lot."

"What did she risk?"

"She did it without her husband's approval."

"I get that. Did she make a commitment to moving in with you? Isn't that what you truly want?"

Once again I couldn't answer definitively. Ms. Tiener pointed out that Lynn had made a financial investment with fringe benefits. She encouraged me to make a list with the headings: *I am, I need, and I want.* She cautioned me not to list a person to fill my needs or wants. Her closing words were, "Everyone has her own list, whether she is conscious of it or not. We all have expectations. In a healthy relationship those expectations are out in the open, and they're either agreed upon or a compromise is made that works for both parties. The compromises should never be overly weighted to only one person. A healthy ratio is 80/20. If you're fortunate and your natures mesh 80 percent of the time, then you each have to compromise only ten percent to make it work."

I left with my brain humming. I had to move out of my apartment this weekend. William, Dick, and Lynn had all agreed to help. Each of us had an agenda. William's was to get my stuff cleared out. Lynn's was to be helpful. Dick's was to keep an eye on us. Mine was to be home.

Sunday was my first night alone in the house. The night was very dark. Countless stars blanketed the sky with tiny glow lights just like they had in the mountains. Parker stayed close to my side. Sleep came easily after the exertions of the day.

The following morning I dove into the task Ms. Tiener had assigned. The exercise brought forth an entire page of scribbling. Under the heading *I am* it was easy. The other two were not so easy. In truth, I realized that I did expect Lynn to meet almost all my needs. I also realized that she had positioned herself in the company to be at my beck and call. If I needed something, she would appear. If I had a question, she searched out the answer and brought it to me. I began to see that her ability to caretake so impeccably was her method of control.

I had been convinced our love for each other was destiny. Perhaps it had actually been by design, whether mine or Lynn's, was what I needed to discover. When she went along with buying the ranch, I thought it was proof of our love. Dr. Waterford's word rang in my ears—clarity. After conquering a life-threatening illness, I could no longer settle for anything less than complete devotion. The surprise revelation I uncovered from the lists was that the commitment I'd been seeking wasn't to me, but to life, and from that stems devotion to a person. And I had to start with myself. The moment when I held that gun in my hand and felt the power to take my life, but chose not to, was the moment I committed to this life and its wonders.

Never one to hesitate once I knew what needed to be done, I drove to the office. Paula was at her desk when I arrived. She had Nathan beside her in a Moses baby basket. She greeted me.

"Honey, why are you back here so soon?" I asked.

"I need to get out of the house," she said. "Jamie is driving me nuts. I can't breathe."

I grinned. "Like mother, like daughter. I'm looking for Lynn."

Paula cocked her head. "Well, I'm sure she'll appear. I swear she follows you like a shadow. I was grateful when you were sick, but now it's annoying."

Lynn appeared, walking down the hall toward us. Paula and I exchanged a conspiratorial glance. I motioned Lynn out the front door of the office. "We need to talk."

We headed toward a path circling a pond, manufactured as a peaceful setting for the office complex.

I eased into my planned speech. "You know I'd love for us to be together all the time."

"Me too, Diana."

"Please listen," I said. "What I need to tell you is that I'm lonely. I want a partner to share my life. I thought that when we bought the ranch together, it was the first step to making that possible. I don't see you changing anything in your life for us. Am I missing something?"

She didn't meet my gaze. "It's just all so new. Somehow I have to juggle what I have with what I want. It has felt like so much pressure. You've got to give me time."

"Oh." I wondered how two or three lunches and one night a week together could be too much pressure.

"I love your wanting me, yet it makes me feel that you want more than I can give," she said. "I feel jerked apart, as though you and Dick are competing for me. I need breathing space."

"What does Dick think is happening with us?"

"He likes and respects you. He wants us all to be friends." Then she made crystal clear what I had been sensing. "I think he fantasizes about a threesome."

My jaw tightened and my stomach churned. We walked in tense silence for a few moments. "And you? Where is your head with this? With all of this?"

"Diana! He's my husband. You're my boss, business partner, and so much more. When you got sick I just couldn't bear to see you so weak. I had to help. I fell in love with you. It's so complicated."

"I will never, absolutely never participate in a threesome with your husband!" I shuddered in disgust, horrified to believe that Lynn might be willing to include Dick in our relationship. The pun wasn't lost on me, but I didn't think Lynn would see the humor. I felt something shift inside. Maybe I needed time, too. "I can give you time and space but, let's set the day that we spend together. I want to stop asking and I don't want either of us to be stressed out."

"That's fine." She smiled. "It would probably help both of us."

She seemed delighted. I was crushed. Hurt as I felt, I had to ask, "Do you still want to stay overnight with me?"

"Diana, of course. How about Wednesdays?" she said as if all her worries had been lifted. "Is that good for you?"

"Yes, fine."

Neither the conversation nor the outcome was what I wanted. Was this part of the ten percent compromise? I didn't think so. But I had agreed to give Lynn time. I would use the time to explore my new world. My body was becoming healthy again. Let the adventure begin.

Our conversation ended a few yards outside the office. Lynn opened the door for me.

"Wednesday at eight at the ranch?" I said as I passed by her.

"Yes," she said and went straight toward her office.

I went past Paula and Nathan without comment. I needed to sit down. I headed straight to my office and had barely reached my chair when Paula, carrying Nathan in his basket, appeared in the doorway.

"What's wrong?" She closed the door, settled Nathan's basket on the floor, and plunked down in the chair across from me. "You walked by me without a word. That's not like you."

"Caught up in my conversation with Lynn, I guess." I took a deep breath.

"Right now, Mom, you don't look so good. You looked fine when you left with Lynn, but not now. What happened?"

"Ranch issues. It'll work out." I met her look and saw the full force of her concern, I tried to smile in reassurance.

"Fine! Whatever!" she exploded. "It's more than ranch issues. What is it with you two?" Then she said what I had been dreading to hear from her. "You know Ben asked me ages ago if you two were lesbians."

"What did you tell him?"

"I said I didn't know. And with you sick, it wasn't really important. Now I'm asking. Are you?" she asked, her eyes still locked on mine.

I hadn't prepared for this. "In the last several months my life has unraveled, as you know, Paula. Right now I'm trying to pick up the pieces and put them together into a new life. One that I want to live."

"Lynn's not right for you. I haven't said anything because," she swallowed, "we needed her. Now that you're getting back to normal, you and I can handle it from here."

Her comments were astute, but I wasn't ready to hear any more. "Paula, these are my decisions to make. Please, no more. Not now."

"I love you, Mom. I can accept anyone, but . . ."

"Anyone? A woman?"

"If that's what you want, but just not her."

"Why not Lynn?" I love my daughter and her love for me was crucial. Was her problem Lynn or her gender?

"I've never liked her."

"I'm aware of that."

"She smothers you. She sits and waits to fulfill your every need. Then she pounces. It makes everyone else feel unimportant." She took a breath. "I feel that she's trying to push me away from you. She makes me feel I'm in competition for your attention. I hate it."

She was right. Lynn had a way of divining my needs. It was uncanny and sometimes eerie. Other employees had voiced their dislike of her condescending tone. I was uncertain and vulnerable on this issue. Defending Lynn was not right. Could I be with Lynn if my children objected? It wasn't their decision to make, although certainly they would be affected by my choice.

"No one can take your place. I love you." I walked around the desk to be near her and kiss my grandson, asleep in her arms. "Look at you two. You've got a big bundle of neediness there. I don't know how this is going to play out, but I'm working on it. Give me some time, and meanwhile put your mothering in that guy's direction."

She was silent. I picked up Nathan and held him. A soft bundle of innocence.

She rose. "I love you, too."

I put Nathan back into her arms. Was there an I-need-time epidemic spreading? Lynn needed time to decide if she wanted to be a lesbian and leave her husband. William needed time to sell our property. I needed finality and monies divided so that I'd be free. Then I could deal with him and the board. Paula needed time to breathe, away from Jamie. I needed time to continue healing and feel triumphant.

# CHAPTER TWENTY-ONE

WHEN I NEXT saw Ms. Tiener I gave her an update on all the current emotional fronts. As usual she told me it's out of my control how other people think, feel, and operate. I only had control over myself. I told her I didn't like being alone. I was ready to expand my lesbian wings.

"Well, there are bookstores, newspapers, restaurants, bars, and coffee shops that cater to gays and lesbians."

"Where? I don't have a clue."

"The newspaper in the waiting room is a good resource. You might enjoy a woman's bookstore for starters. Go with what feels right for you."

I picked up the newspaper on my way out. The weekend was spent reading, journaling, and walking the land. Both Lynn and Paula reached out with a phone call. Neither rushed over to be with me.

The newspaper was mind-boggling, an awakening to a world I hadn't known existed. I was both drawn to it and also scared of it. There were articles about gay harassment, upcoming events, and a story titled, "A Queen's Saga." Advertisements covered a broad spectrum that included bars, tattoos, pornography, coffee shops, sex toys, restaurants, leather shops, jewelry, and massage. The personal ads read like a mysterious code. I tried hard to break it. I'm pretty sure I didn't.

I was an explorer, ready to be drawn into new territory, at least new to me. By the tenth reading the paper was flecked with highlights and notations. A separate page on my legal pad had names, phone numbers, and addresses of interesting places. I decided to stop in at a woman's bookstore on Monday.

The neighborhood seemed quiet. The bookstore was flanked by a restaurant and a kite shop. Private residences were mostly

Victorian in architecture. I parked on the street in front of the bookstore and looked at the window display.

I read the titles: *The Sisterhood, Religion and Sexism, The First Sex.* A woman brushed against my shoulder. "Going in?"

"Ah, yes."

She held the door for me and I entered. Another woman was sitting on a blanket-covered sofa with a cat in her lap. "Can I help you find anything?"

"Just looking."

"If you need anything, just ask."

"Thank you."

I cruised the shelves—history, philosophy, religion, health, biographies, and fiction. It was similar to other bookstores, except that the emphasis was on women. The layout was organized but packed. I heard occasional conversations and laughter in the background as I perused the books.

I had selected a number of books when I came to a room with a heavy purple curtain draped back on both sides of the doorway. The scent of smoky sage lured me in. Beautiful crystallized rock formations sat on black velvet, and an arrangement of pewter wizards, gargoyles, dragons, and other mystical beings were displayed. I liked the magical feel of the room, but decided I had enough to research without adding the spiritual realms to my quest.

I began to make my way to the checkout, noticing racks of records and shelves of cassette tapes from female artists I didn't know. I'd give those more attention on my next visit. Then passing through another door I nearly dropped my books. Posters of women had been attached to the wall, floor, and ceiling. I stared at the sensual images. There were women of all colors, fully clothed and nude, some with tattoos and/or piercings. After studying them for a time, I glanced around, slightly embarrassed. Thankfully I was alone. I turned to head out and stopped. Next to the doorway were shelves filled with a variety of vibrators, condoms, and other sex toys that I secretly craved to examine. Leaving the room, I ran into another woman.

"I'm sorry," I mumbled, trying not to appear out of place.

"Nice room, huh?" was her reply.

Not being able to think of a suitable response, I merely nodded and moved toward the front of the store. Had I been crazy to come here? No! The bookstore was different. I'd been exposed to more than I'd anticipated. My naiveté shocked me and made me feel a little afraid, or was it exhilarated? I needed to leave.

The woman from the couch was now behind the counter. I placed the stack of books next to the cash register, reading the titles to myself as she rang them up: *Our Bodies, Ourselves, Now That You Know, Women on Women, Rubyfruit Jungle.*

"Did you find everything you wanted?"

"Yes, thank you," I said, knowing my selection of books revealed a lot about me. I pulled my credit card, hesitated, and wondered if I should use it for this kind of purchase, and slipped it back in its slot. When the total was more than my cash, I resorted to the card rather than put back any books.

In the car, I took a deep breath and drove back to the office, the posters vivid in my mind. Some I found distasteful, but there were a few that were rather beautiful. Would every woman, if she were honest, say the same, or was this an indicator of my lesbian nature? I didn't know. Couldn't we just be sexual beings, with no labels or stigma attached?

My expedition to the bookstore had been pleasant and erotic. It seemed a safe place to explore what I considered my new frontier. I had books stashed in my purse, beneath my bed, and under the car seat. I stole every available minute to read. My imagination soared.

I felt constricted, which was disheartening. I was learning so much and I wanted to share it with Lynn. Her absence was painful. Often I had to fight the urge to call her; somehow I sensed this was a private journey.

Lynn was all smiles at work. She kept her usual post at my office door, ready should I want anything. Her need for space, at least at the office, wasn't apparent. I loved the attention, I always had, but now it made the situation harder for me. How was I supposed to act?

I TOLD MS. Tiener I had scoped out the bookstore. I shared my disappointment that the evening I spent with Lynn did not include any lively discussion or rapt explorations of my discoveries. Ms. Tiener in her succinct way spelled it out for me. Lynn was a part-time lover who didn't want or need any involvement with a supportive lesbian or bi-sexual community. She encouraged me to continue my research. I thought about it for a moment. She was right.

I pulled the marked-up newspaper from my purse. "I don't understand the personals."

"I see you've read that paper," she said with a chuckle. "Let me help you." She quickly deciphered various acronyms that described gender, color, and sexual identity.

The hour was over. I had direction. I had the personals to explore. Conquering my fear and following through, or not, was up to me. I decided to take the bull by the horns when I left Ms. Tiener. I drove to the Broadway Coffee House. Brave as I was in most circumstances, my knees were shaking as I walked through the doorway. The tables were nearly filled with same-sex couples.

"Can I help you?"

I looked and saw that the offer came from a wicked purple hairdo standing behind the counter. The bouncer-looking server and I checked each other out from top to bottom.

I glanced at the handwritten menu hanging on the wall behind the counter. "Coffee, please."

Hairdo handed me a cup of coffee and said, "One dollar, please," in a husky voice that defied my ability to discern gender.

I paid while being told, "Cream, sugar, cinnamon, and cocoa are at the end of the counter. Help yourself."

I tried to calm my panic as I shook cinnamon into my cup. It spilled on the counter. To leave with the coffee would have been cowardly. I forced myself to sit at the only empty table.

I sipped, taking in the combat boots, tennis shoes, army pants, blue jeans, sweatpants, and denim workshirts. Body language was free and bold, almost defiant. Everyone seemed confident and self-assured as they touched, nudged, patted, and hugged one another. I was ignored, which let me drink and watch. They were comfortable showing affection and being themselves. It was something I deeply wanted for myself.

I was aware that my dark green pantsuit and heels stood out. My style was corporate polish. After seeing these free-spirited, all-out-there women, I doubted I would fit in. I wasn't sure I could. I envied their boldness.

"Would you like anything else?" The words were inches from my ear.

"I don't think so." I looked up and saw a young woman. Her hair was on top of her head in a hair spout, and she wore a t-shirt, jeans, and hot pink tennis shoes.

"Friday night crowd," she said. "The afternoons are quieter. You can play games, read, and socialize."

"That might be better," I said. "I just came from work. I feel overdressed."

"No dress code here. There are enough rules outside that door. In here you can be yourself."

I smiled. "Thank you."

"You're welcome." She moved to another customer.

As I got up to leave I heard her call, "Do come back."

"I will," I said, a polite reflex.

Her friendliness comforted me somewhat, but it had been a grueling experience. My knees nearly buckled as I pushed the door open. The fresh air was cool against my perspiring body.

In the car my nervousness became uncontrollable giggling until thoughts of Lynn surfaced. Why couldn't I share this with her? She could make love to me but unless we were at the ranch, we didn't talk freely or touch openly.


THE WEEKEND BROUGHT William, Dick, Lynn, and a truckload of rabbit equipment. My repeated instructions about how I wanted the cages went unheeded. It was pointless. The men had a game plan and followed it.

Lynn tried to create opportunities for us to be alone. I was feeling churlish and no longer wanted to play the secret touching game with her. I chose to brave the male chauvinism and busied myself near where they were working. When the lights, water tank, and cages were all installed, we stood and admired the job. I wish I could have felt genuine pleasure at our accomplishment, but I didn't. I was angry that I hadn't stood up for myself.

They finally left and I spent the evening scanning the personals to see if anything attracted me. I spotted an ad that not only struck me as personable and safe, it also stated they were looking for a business partner to help develop an animal care business. I decided to call in the morning.

The woman who answered said her name was Samantha. She sounded sweet, not young and not old. What would she look like? What would she wear? What should I wear? If I was totally put off I could leave. It would be fine.

I found the restaurant where we had decided to meet. Looking around inside, I saw a woman nearly my age already seated. Her hair was not pink, purple, or spiked. I gulped as I walked. Was that her? I told myself to stand up straight and look ahead, not at the ground. My grandfather's advice, I wondered what he would have thought about this meeting.

"Hello, Samantha? I'm Diana." I extended my hand.

She took it. "Hi, Diana." She had a warm, firm grip.

My heart was pounding, throat was constricted and mouth was dry. We exchanged small talk about the weather and traffic.

We looked over the menu. She offered insights on what to order, having eaten there before. My nerves settled enough for me to stop bouncing my foot.

After we ordered she told her story. "My partner of 24 years and I have a home, lots of animals, and numerous longtime friends. We're comfortable, perhaps stagnant. We've been saving money for years to buy property and offer spa care for dogs while people go on vacation."

I relaxed some. Though she'd admitted to some boredom, she appeared happy, settled, and responsible. I told her about the ranch. The more we engaged in conversation, the more I appreciated Samantha's humor and keen mind. I enjoyed her candor. I told her about my identity crisis and said that I was seeking kindred spirits to find some understanding. She said it would be a pleasure to introduce me to more kindred spirits.

As we parted she turned. "We'd love to come out to your ranch and you're welcome to come to our place."

"I would be delighted," I said.

We agreed to call and set a date. I drove back to the office ruminating about Samantha. She was polite, knowledgeable, and professional. I was looking forward to spending more time with her and to meeting her partner.

It was mid-afternoon when I returned to the office. Paula looked up and smiled. Nathan was asleep in his basket. Would she and Ben still love me if I came out as a lesbian? Should I maintain secrecy or could I endure potential ridicule? I didn't know. I was surprised to realize I felt OK with not knowing.

# CHAPTER TWENTY-TWO

TODAY I WAS actually able to talk to my son. When I called Trent's house periodically, either his mom or dad would answer. I had become uncomfortable when I talked to them. I didn't know if my son was deliberately avoiding me or if, as they told me, he was always out.

He sounded hurried. "What's up, Mom?"

"It's good to hear your voice," I said.

"Is everything OK?"

"Yes, I'm fine. I've moved. I'm sure your sister told you. I bought a ranch property and would love to have you come out."

"Sure."

"How about this weekend?"

"I'm busy. My friends and I are taking a course to learn how to make beer."

"That sounds like fun. You should bring some out so I can try it." I paused to see if he would respond. He didn't. "We started raising rabbits again."

"Who's we?"

"Lynn is helping me."

"Is she living with you?"

"No, I'm here with Parker."

He was silent. I waited.

"Ben, I'm sorry about all of this. I know it's been hard on you, too."

I listened to him breathe. Did I lose my son?

"I want you in my life," I said, trying not to sound desperate.

"I'll think about it, Mom."

"Think about what?"

"Coming out to see you."

"Just let me know when." I was relieved that he didn't pursue the Lynn issue. I didn't know what Paula had told him. I realized there was nothing else to say but, "I love you, son."

"I love you too, Mom. I gotta go."

He hung up. Had I been cut out of his life because of the illness? The divorce? Lynn? Did he think I had abandoned him? I was hoping to spend more time with him and ask him these questions. I'd have to continue relying on Paula to keep me informed. She liked that. She had an unquenchable need to be needed. Ben and I were more alike. We liked our autonomy. Perhaps that's all this was, his declaration of independence. I didn't want to think I could lose my son because of my sexual preference.


SAMANTHA BECAME LIKE a mother duck teaching her giddy duckling the ways of the new world. I paddled along behind her to movies, lunches, coffeehouses, and comedy clubs. Every outing was an experience in gay and lesbian culture. Her partner, Ann, and their friends were just as generous, introducing me to their world.

Socializing took the edge off my loneliness. I explained that I was involved with an uncertain, non-social, lesbian-hating, married-to-a-man, part-time woman love partner. Well, I watered it down so I wouldn't appear to be such a fool. And I was a fool over her. But I'd promised to give her time to work out her issues. She was there for me when I was at my most vulnerable. Maybe this was her most vulnerable time.

Early one morning Lynn met me in the parking lot just as I pulled in. "I tried calling you last night. Until ten." I was slightly annoyed at her tone and at the same time impressed that she had the nerve.

"I was out with friends. Something wrong?"

"I missed you. I wanted to talk."

"Let's talk now. I have a few minutes before Paula and I go to a business lunch."

"You're always off meeting someone."

"You know the next board meeting is looming. I need to strengthen my position and vet my allies so I can oust William." Since the divorce we had become territorial animals, circling each other, preparing for the next attack. I managed to keep him busy with design projects but our interaction was wary. The next board meeting would be our final showdown.

"I'm a shareholder," Lynn said. "Why can't I come with you to these meetings instead of Paula?"

This was the first time Lynn voiced her competitiveness with my daughter. I wasn't surprised. I was disturbed.

"I wouldn't have thought I needed to garner your alliance."

"I'm sorry. I don't mean to be so pathetic. I hate it when I call and there's no answer, or you've got guests."

"Lynn, I'm sorry you're upset but I'm not going to wait alone at home for you to call or visit. I did that. It's not fun. I'm keeping busy so I don't pressure you."

I waited for her to respond. She gazed off in silence. We walked back toward the office. We entered and I stopped to talk to Paula. Lynn moved on, seemingly in a trance.

"What's with her?" Paula asked.

I shrugged. "She has some issues to work out."

"I'll say," Paula retorted.

That evening the phone rang at eight. I nudged Parker from around my feet and went to answer.

"Diana?" It was Lynn. She was crying.

"What's wrong?"

"I miss you so much. I want to be with you. We're meant for each other. I don't want you out and about without me."

Was this it? Was she going to commit to a relationship with me? I was alert. Ready.

"Dick sits at home waiting for me to fix meals," she complained. "There's no appreciation, just demands. And the boys are just like him. I'm sick of it. I told him I love you. He didn't get it. So I told him that we love each other and want to be together. Without him."

I was so stunned I couldn't utter a word. Had she just now made that clear to him?

"He walked out, yelling that he had put up with enough of our feminist bullshit and that I had to end it with you now."

"You just now told him all of this?"

"Yes."

"I thought he knew."

"He didn't. He's mad, Diana. He's really mad."

That explained a lot. My mind reeled. She had him at bay, like me. She had led both of us on all this time. He must be furious. I was appalled. I didn't know whether to laugh or cry.

"Diana? Are you there?"

"Yes," I said, jolted back to the conversation.

"After that," she went on, "I called my sister."

My spinning thoughts halted and turned in this new direction. She rarely spoke of her staunchly catholic sister. "And how did that go?"

"I told her about our connection, that I truly believe we're soulmates and that I love you more than I've ever known was possible." Only gulping noises came through the phone.

I smiled at the courage Lynn had shown. "Are you OK?"

"Yes," she whispered.

"Do you want to come out here?"

She didn't respond.

"Should I come and get you?" I waited another moment. "Are you there?"

"I'm here. I just don't know what to do." She unleashed another torrent. "My sister says it's wrong. It's against the teachings of the Church. She asked how I could even consider throwing away years of marriage for sin and damnation. She said I should be grateful that Dick gives me more freedom than most husbands. I'm breaking apart. Living without you is hell." Her piercing cries were like the wailing of a siren. I didn't know what to do except hold the phone away from my ear and pet Parker. Finally she wore herself out and said she'd talk with me tomorrow.

Lynn's phone call and the board meeting on the horizon increased my usual night restlessness. I got up before dawn and went to the office. When slivers of sunlight peeked through the blinds, I went to raise them. I saw Lynn pull into the parking lot. She stumbled getting out of the car and walked slowly to the door. I met her in the hallway and we walked to her office. She was spent.

"He ordered me not to come here," she said, slumping into her chair. "He's upset in a way I've never seen before." I closed the door to her office as her voice rose. "I had to come. I have a job to do. I had to see you."

"Lynn, you took a stand when you helped to buy the ranch. You said that your heart and soul told you we should be together. You can make that happen now. Come live with me. We can work out the rest together."

There was a glimmer of a smile as she looked up at me. "Do you think so?" Her lips were cracked and her breath was stale.

"Yes."

"You're not scared?"

"No, Lynn, this is what I want."

She sat up. "I'll talk with him."

What the hell did that mean? Why would she talk with him? I decided to go back home. I couldn't witness the drag-yourself-through-broken-glass process of ending a long marriage, especially when I had an attachment to the outcome.

She joined me later that day at the ranch. I hugged her, not letting go for some time. She sobbed. I didn't know what to say. Her being here in my arms was enough for now. How long had I wanted this? I waited for her to speak, feeling it best.

I massaged her neck and shoulders. She was silent. I couldn't stop myself. "Talk to me," I urged.

"I can't. It's too fresh, too mangled. I have to sort it out."

I took her hand and led her to bed. We lay fully clothed with her head on my shoulder and my arms holding her tightly. I could be with her now in all her pain and uncertainty, as she had been with me through mine. When exhaustion overcame her tears I relaxed my arms and stroked her hair. She did not stir.

The morning light illuminated Lynn's tear-blotched face. Her hands trembled as she tried to apply makeup to mask the dark shadows evident under her eyes.

"You don't have to go to work today," I said.

"We should go," Lynn said after a final glance at her reflection in the mirror.

We walked to our respective cars. I hovered beside mine. "I can drive."

She went to hers and opened the door. "Will Saturday be OK with you?"

"Are you going back to him tonight?" I was astonished.

"You've been through this with William. Separating is hard. There are a lot of complications. We need to work some things out, but I'd like to be with you on Saturday."

"OK, fine." I was totally confused but had lived with worse. I considered not going into work, but I didn't want to shirk my duties or leave Lynn alone with her demons. We left for the office at the same time in our own cars.

Paula took one look at me as I entered. "Rough night?"

"You could say that." I moved toward Lynn's office.

"She looks beat to hell, too."

Her office door was closed. I knocked and without waiting for a response, I entered. She was on the phone, not speaking. I walked behind her and gently rubbed her shoulders. Then I left. She knew I was there for her. I had made my point.

The light on her phone extension stayed lit most of the morning. She didn't call me on the intercom or emerge from her office.

I didn't leave for lunch but eventually I had to go to an appointment with Dr. Waterford. I got into my car and started driving the familiar route. I wondered if Lynn would be at the office waiting for me when I returned. William was emotionally abusive, his drinking was intolerable and yet I still had difficulty breaking away until he attacked my son. Dick, as far as I knew, hadn't shown physical or emotional violence toward Lynn or their sons. Her decision had to be driven by her own will. I suppose we all have dark places we don't want to shine light on. I turned the radio on to keep from caving to my obsession, the psychological assessment of Lynn and me.

A local news talk show was airing. I reached over to change the station. I wanted music not misery. I stopped when I heard the male host say, "What about the lady here in Denver whose doctor failed to notice a Lyme test that read three times higher than normal. She was incapacitated for over three months because doctors couldn't determine what was wrong with her." He had my attention as he went on. "Talk about a medical screw up!"

"Imagine the hell she's been through," the female host said. "According to the Center for Disease Control, if left untreated, the Lyme bacteria spreads causing a variety of musculoskeletal, neurological, and cardiac problems. Over years it can lead to arthritis, nerve, or brain damage."

"So we're describing full body deterioration just like the Rocky Mountain Spotted Fever you can get from the dog tick," her co-host replied.

"I think the tick that carries Lyme is called the deer tick," the female host said.

"There should be a diagram of menacing ticks to watch out for on all hiking trails."

"What are you gonna do, hike with a magnifying glass?"

"Are you kidding me? The great outdoors can stay outside. Too many dangerous critters and most of 'em you can't see."

"CSU claims that no human cases of Lyme disease have originated in Colorado."

"Really. I'm sure the woman who is currently suffering with it will argue that statistic."

"The CDC maintains that the test for Lyme can be inconclusive, so doctors have a difficult time diagnosing. A surefire test to detect it has yet to be developed."

The male host concluded the segment with the caustic comment, "I'm sure she'll feel better knowing that." They moved on to other news.

Stunned, I turned the radio off. Was it me they were talking about? What did he say about a Lyme test not read properly? How did this get on the news? I shook my head to clear it so I could drive. I was already in the medical office parking lot. I wasn't sure how I got there, but I eased into a slot, got out, and locked my doors.

I headed to Dr. Waterford's office. I could feel myself heating up and rage boiled in my veins like molten lava. I entered his waiting room and walked right into his office, bypassing his receptionist. She rose from her chair and came after me. I opened his door.

"You misread my Lyme test?"

He waved off his receptionist, stood, and came from behind his desk to face me. "We did have a problem with our diagnostic reading. The calibrations were not set properly. The CDC collaborated with the Association of State and Territorial Public Health Labs to standardize testing protocols for better reliability. They have been doing audits around the country. We submitted the past six months of lab work and that was when we were notified that your Lyme titer was positive."

I gaped. Here I stood, a medical device engineer who designed an intricate piece of equipment that moderated the flow of blood through a human heart. How was I to make sense of an equipment malfunction that almost cost me my life? And for all I knew caused long term damage. What kind of fate was this?

Dr. Waterford came toward me with a worried expression.

I stepped back. "What if they hadn't caught this error?"

"I can't answer that."

"Have you already been advised by an attorney?"

He was silent. My anger turned to bone-weary disappointment. Here was another man that I had trusted who failed me. My legs were turning to jelly. I had to get out of there.

"You'll be hearing from my attorney, as well," I snapped as I strode through his waiting room and out the door.

I arrived back in my office parking lot. Lynn's car was gone. Paula was standing at the door. Her mom radar was highly tuned. She held the door for me. "Mom, what's wrong?"

I recounted my afternoon as she trailed behind me. I could feel her start to bristle. She exploded in language that would make rapper lyrics seem tame. I landed in my desk chair. Tears of outrage and disappointment fell.

Paula took my hands. "Do you want me to call your attorney?"

"Tomorrow morning," I said. "I'm exhausted. I just want to go home."


LYNN CAME TO the ranch on Saturday. I didn't know how she managed it, and I didn't ask. We briefly discussed the radio broadcast, my meeting with Dr. Waterford, and my decision not to pursue a lawsuit based on meeting with the attorney. I told her that I would have to be the initiatory plaintiff in a class action suit, a responsibility that I didn't want. I did not want to waste one more minute battling with a tick. And even though I'd suffered from the mistake, the debacle had been resolved. My attorney's advice that my health could be compromised by a long and arduous case cinched my decision. She wanted me to fight. I told her it wasn't the fight I wanted to win. She dropped it.

We managed to have a great day. I agreed to her proposal to spend Wednesdays and Saturdays together. Her argument was "I need time to work out an arrangement about the boys and our finances." I had thought this was already in process, but her recent confession proved that to be wrong.

We had more time together. When it still seemed as though she was no closer to making a complete commitment to me, much less accepting a lesbian identity, I started to gently pry. Being patient didn't mean I had to be left in the dark. Mostly I heard, "We're working it out," or "I'm here now, can't we just enjoy our time together." When I became more persistent, I discovered there was no definitive plan for divorce, division of property, or custody.

I endured Lynn's indecisiveness for as long as I could. I had no exclusivity with her. She was still sexually active with Dick. A future with her was yet to be determined. Meanwhile, I had turned down dates with women who had made peace with their sexual identity. They were already able to make a commitment if the right person came along. I wanted it to be Lynn. We'd been through so much. Love was there. I knew it, but I couldn't force it. This was a hard truth learned from my invaluable sessions with Ms. Tiener. I decided it was time for me to date.

# CHAPTER TWENTY-THREE

SAMANTHA SET ME up with an aerobics instructor named Sue. She was to be my date for my coming out party, which Samantha had orchestrated. She and her friends vowed to take me to every gay and lesbian bar they knew. I couldn't wait. I was ready for some play time unencumbered by both Lynn's prissy judgment and William's pompous self-aggrandizing. This night was for me.

Our first stop was a gay nightclub. We entered a small foyer where we checked our coats. An elaborate Victorian bar reigned over the crowded main room. Two wide archways with ornamental molding led to the dance floor. Wainscoting lined the lower portion of the walls. Mirrors paneled the top. Strobe lights and a glittering disco ball made the room pulse. Gay and lesbian couples were talking, dancing, cuddling, arguing, and kissing. They were free to be themselves. And so was I.

Samantha knew I didn't drink. She understood my health complications and had told me that several of her friends would drink soda or coffee throughout the evening. But my drug treatment was now completed. I was feeling very alive, a little frightened and ready to throw caution to the winds. I ordered a kamikaze. My plan was to sip it slowly over the next few hours. Samantha looked at me quizzically.

"It's OK," I said. "The treatments are over and I haven't needed any pain pills."

"Go for it, lady," she said.

We pulled two tables together to accommodate Samantha and Ann, Marta and Gwen, Mary, Pam, Kathy, Ellen, my date Sue, and me. We got comfortable and our drinks arrived.

Samantha proposed a toast. "To Diana, to her coming out. May she find what she's looking for."

"May it be me," Ellen said, catching my eye. She turned to Sue. "Be nice to her; we're watching." Everyone laughed. I was polite to Sue and she to me, but the chemistry wasn't there. We soon turned our attentions to others.

The second place was a small bar called *Sisters* in a depressed neighborhood. We sat at two tables adjacent to the dance floor. There was no way to get up or down without knocking chairs with another table. Cigarette burns marked the old hardwood floors. Smoke hovered in vaporous clouds, the stench as thick as mist. Normally my skin would have been crawling and I'd have left for air, but not tonight. Perhaps it was the alcohol. Perhaps it was being surrounded by bold and vivacious women, unafraid to express their feelings and desires. Indeed, I seemed to be the prize of the evening.

A woman in metal-studded leather pants with tattoos running the length of her arm sauntered over from the bar and asked me to dance. Her scent of Old Spice surprised me. I was searching for a kind rebuff when Samantha said gruffly, "She's with me."

I chuckled after the woman walked away and gently nudged Samantha. "Thanks."

"Not your type, Diana?" Marta quizzed.

"Am I your type?" Pam asked.

"Perhaps you'd dance with me?" Mary said.

I blushed and sipped my drink.

"I said she's with me," Samantha asserted and then turned to me. "Would you care to dance?"

I looked from her to Ann. She nodded.

It was a slow dance and Samantha pulled me close. I was stiff and felt claustrophobic.

"It's OK, Diana. It's just a dance."

I relaxed. I ended up dancing with every woman at our table before we left for the next bar.

We drove across town. Music could be heard even in the parking lot. We all traipsed into a pulsating, smoke-shrouded cave packed with women. It seemed as though I had fallen into an ancient world. The thrill of entering a space devoted solely to women shot bubbles down my spine that exploded with an effervescent gush. Ann guided us to the only table available. When we weren't dancing or roaming the cave, the eight of us shared three chairs and sipped on drinks from the assortment at our table. Mostly we danced.

Every time we moved we were brushed into someone. Many introduced themselves. Some gave me their phone numbers. I was more comfortable with Samantha and her friends, but I did dance with other women. I caught a glance from a slim woman with almond eyes. When we caught each other's eyes she turned away. She never did ask me to dance.

During my last dance with Samantha, with my head resting on her shoulder, she said, "I believe you're quite drunk."

I raised my head. I felt dizzy. "I believe you're right." I nuzzled into her neck. I was close enough to detect a hint of orange. I truly loved being with women.

Leaving the bar, I found the cool fresh air to be a welcome shock. Samantha and Ann took me to a coffee shop a few blocks away. My pupils contracted from the bright lights. I breathed in the aroma of coffee and cigarettes. To me, the smell was more tolerable compared to the bars we had just visited. I was sure I would have to strip out of my party clothes before I entered my house.

Samantha, her friends, and everyone I had met bar hopping had been informative. Opinions differed on all issues but the cardinal rule was to never out anyone else. Identity issues could be a matter of life and death. Disclosure was a personal choice. Unlike race, which cannot be hidden, sexual preference isn't necessarily obvious. The places I had been taken to were considered sacred. It was safe to abandon the masquerade there that had to be kept up in most other areas of life. I thought the discrimination suffered by gay and lesbians intensified the sense of camaraderie I witnessed and felt. Ironically the corporate world that had been my social orbit was competitive, hypocritical, and misogynist. Why had I felt more comfortable in that world? Why did I feel compelled to prove myself to such people?

Morning brought a headache and light spasms. I would have to take it easy. Lynn arrived midmorning full of energy, reminding me of Parker, who was racing all over the place, gleeful that I was home for the day.

"What should we do today?" Lynn chirpily asked.

"I'm not feeling well," I said.

Lynn immediately turned into emergency nurse mode. "What's wrong?"

I smiled. Her deep concern for me was a cornerstone of our love. "It's nothing medical. Just a hangover."

Her eyes narrowed. "You were drinking?"

"A bit too much."

"Alone?"

"No."

"Who was with you? Did they know you shouldn't be drinking?"

"Lynn, It's OK. I was with friends. I had a great time. I'm not complaining. I just need to take it easy."

"What friends? Do I know them?"

"No one you know."

"Lesbians!"

I could almost see the lightbulb flash in her head. I didn't want to hurt her feelings, and I could see that she was not going to let this go. She was both fascinated and repelled by her desire, similar to her attraction to Ms. Tiener. I didn't have enough stamina to handle her self-righteous queries.

I headed for the barn and sauntered over to a pile of straw bales. She followed. I sat and leaned my aching head against them. A whiff of rabbit droppings filtered into my nostrils. I suppressed my gag reflex.

She noticed my distress. "I'll feed and water the rabbits."

I nodded, glad she was occupied. Just thinking about last night was almost as good as the actual experience. I knew deep down that this was who I was. I wrapped my arms around my knees. Dancing with women had been so freeing.

"Do you want to go inside?" Lynn asked, interrupting my reverie. She offered her hand. "Has something upset you?" I took it and we walked to the house together, Parker bouncing along with us.

"Why do you ask?"

"You were drinking. Were you depressed?"

"I'm fine. It's been a long time since I've had alcohol and it just hit me hard."

I pitched in to get lunch ready and tidy up afterward. I stifled amused smiles whenever thoughts from the previous evening tickled my mind. The day seemed to drag. I wanted to rest and reflect.

When we went to bed I stroked her breasts. Her skin was soft and warm. Nibbling at her neck, I smelled her apple scent and was reminded of Samantha's scent of orange. Did all women smell of fruit? I drew in a second whiff. I played with her pleasure zones, moved her to wanting, and then watched her explode.

My skin tingled wherever her fingers stroked. I felt her lips on my neck. I wondered how I smelled to her. I pictured myself dancing with all the different women. We were close. Very close. We wanted to be closer. There was no shame. I let myself go. An ecstatic release.

"I love the way you touch me," Lynn said. "I was afraid you weren't feeling up to it." Then she rolled over and was soon sound asleep.

I was no longer uncertain about my sexuality. Whether Lynn was with me on that or not didn't matter. I wasn't ready for a bold declaration, but I wouldn't lie about it. I was a lesbian.

ON MONDAY AT the office, Paula announced a caller. "Mom, there's a Samantha on line four."

"Yes, thanks," I said, clicking over to that line. "Hello, Samantha."

"Hello, just called to see how you are."

"I'm good. Thank you so much for Friday night. It was just what I needed."

"So you'd be up for doing it again?"

"I'd love to. With less alcohol and fewer smoke-filled clubs."

Samantha laughed. "How about dinner tomorrow, just you and I?"

"Great, what time?"

"Can I pick you up at five?"

"Perfect."

The next day, minutes before Samantha was due to arrive, I walked to Paula's desk at the front entry. I set my briefcase on the floor. "Samantha's coming by and we're going to dinner."

Paula eyed me. "OK."

I had a perfect view of the parking lot and was poised to make a fast exit. Samantha drove up, and I started to head for the door.

"Are you leaving?" I heard Lynn call out. She was bustling down the hallway.

"Yes."

"Bye, Mom," Paula said and then with a glance at Lynn, she added a little snidely, "Have a nice time."

I'd hoped to be a bit more discreet, but Samantha was already out of her car smiling broadly. My see-you-tomorrow comments sailed behind me as I went out the door. Samantha opened the passenger door for me. Glancing through the windshield, I could see Lynn and Paula watching. Samantha saw them, looked at my face, pushed the play button on the car stereo, backed up, and we sped away. I leaned my head back and listened to Billie Holiday croon love and betrayal songs on the way to the restaurant.

We entered the restaurant she had chosen. It was a romantic sanctuary. Candles flickered everywhere. Fresh flowers adorned crisp white tablecloths. After we were seated, sparkling goblets were filled with water, and the waiter carefully placed menus and the wine list on the table. Then he seemed to evaporate.

"Do you want to order a bottle of wine?" Samantha asked.

I smiled ruefully. "I would love to, but I'm still recovering from the other night." I perused the menu. "Do you have a recommendation?"

"Do you like fettuccine Alfredo?" Samantha asked. "It's divine here."

"That sounds good."

A basket with freshly baked bread quickly appeared. "Are you ready to order?" our Houdini-like waiter asked. Samantha ordered. The waiter gathered our menus and once again disappeared.

"What is your commitment to Lynn?" Samantha asked.

Startled, I took a sip of water before I answered. "Essentially, she can't make a commitment to me until she sorts things out with her husband." I met Samantha's gaze. "She knows I'm socializing with other people."

"Ann and I are committed. She recognizes that I have needs she can't meet and allows for that. She's more homey, quiet, and private. Friday night was a real social stretch for her." She offered me the bread before helping herself. "I tell her everything. It's almost as if we're more friends than lovers, though we are that, too."

"I hope to have that kind of relationship someday."

"Ann suggested I ask you out to dinner. She's aware that I'm attracted to you."

"She is? You are?"

She laughed. "I doubt there was anyone at our table Friday who didn't see that. Except you."

How naive had I been? She had protected me from undesirable advances and made certain I was never left alone or without a drink. "But you set me up with Sue!"

"Didn't work, did it?"

"No."

"Well . . ."

We laughed.

"Did Sue know what you were up to?" I asked after a few moments.

"It wasn't intentional. I wanted you to have a good coming-out party. I thought maybe she'd interest you, but as the evening progressed I was glad she didn't."

She took my hands and held them between hers. "Am I being too honest?"

"Too forward perhaps, but never too honest." I smiled. "Your intensity is flattering."

"When we danced the other night it took all I had not to kiss you. I didn't want to upset you."

"Upset *me*! What about Ann?"

"Ann would have been fine. But I wasn't sure you would be OK. I didn't want to do anything to offend you."

"Oh," I said, thinking back. How would I have reacted? I wasn't sure. "I may have freaked, especially since I didn't know how Ann felt."

"Can I kiss you now?"

"Right here in public?" I looked around. I hadn't noticed that the restaurant clientele were all same-sex couples. "There's a table between us!"

She moved her chair closer, put an arm behind me, and pulled me to her. She tilted my head to meet her kiss. It was long and luscious. When we parted, I savored the lingering sensations she left on my lips. Her boldness excited me.

Our waiter appeared and placed beautifully embellished plates of creamy fettuccini in front of us. He offered fresh ground pepper and parmesan cheese. The meal was exquisite.

Samantha had brought an astrology book to show me how compatible we were. I was charmed. An aspiring poet, she shared one of her most recent poems for which I was the inspiration. We shared hungry kisses all the way back to the ranch.

I disconnected the phone without listening to messages and lit the fireplace. Within moments we were lying naked on the rug by the fire. Her caresses were gentle, her hands skilled. We explored each other, touching, tasting, and delving into the mounds and folds of our bodies. We left no territory uncharted. Sated, we lay in each other's arms until 4 a.m. We dressed and made our way back to town. Her shift started at 6 a.m.

# CHAPTER TWENTY-FOUR

I WAS WORKING in my office.

"You look happy, Mom," Paula greeted.

I glanced up.

"You must be feeling better to be here so early!" Since my illness she had been beating me to work each morning. I felt her close scrutiny.

It was true that my night with Samantha had definitely released a lot of pent-up frustration from the past months. Uncomplicated sex is such a good balm. I tried not to blush. "I wanted to get some paperwork done before the day erupts into chaos."

"Mom. You're blushing."

"What do you mean?"

"Were you out all night?"

My hesitation was enough for her to burst out laughing. "Well, you certainly rattled Lynn's cage."

"Close the door."

"Why? No one is here yet." She did as I asked. "I've wanted to talk to you, anyway."

Uh oh, I said silently. "OK."

"Mom, you deserve better. Lynn is never going to leave Dick. I'm sorry. I want you to be happy. I just can't stand her."

"And what if it's not Lynn but still a woman?"

"Are you a lesbian now?"

"Yes."

"It's weird. I mean you've always been with a man."

"Paula, I'm done with men."

"I have a girlfriend who's a lesbian." I prepared myself the way all mothers do who hear a confession from their grown children that you wish they would keep to themselves forever. Paula continued with her revelation. "We went out once, not like a date, just girls going out. She took me to a lesbian bar and I met some of her friends. We had a lot to drink and she tried to kiss me. I told her I'm not into girls. She never did it again."

I wondered if I had been to the same bar. I had no idea what to say. We stared at each other, both of us slightly uneasy. Suddenly two loud knocks sounded on the door. It swung open.

Lynn appeared, distraught. "I need to speak with you now!"

Paula jumped from her chair. "I'll see you later, Mom." She sent a contemptuous look toward Lynn and gave me a raised eyebrow. "Let me know if you need me." Then she shut the door behind her.

Lynn stood in front of my desk like a drill sergeant. "Who was that woman you left with yesterday? Where did you go? I tried calling you all night."

"Lynn, stop."

"Did you sleep with her?" Her face was blotchy and she looked disheveled. It was not a normal look for her.

"Have you been up all night?" I asked.

"Of course. I was worried sick."

"Why?" I asked.

Did this finally blow her out of her indecisive stance? I waited with butterflies in my stomach, hoping that I would finally hear everything I'd been waiting so long for.

She took a step back, her shoulders slumped and she threw a look of surrender toward me. "My sister's right. I can't throw away my marriage for this." She marched to the door, wrenched it open, stood in the doorway, and faced me again to deliver her final verdict. "I don't want my life to be so hard. I'm out." Then she slammed the door behind her.

She hadn't fought for me, she'd walked. Before I had time to sort out how I felt, the door reopened. William appeared, a sheaf of papers in hand.

"Lovers quarrel?" he quipped.

I should have gone home as Paula suggested. I braced myself, ignoring his insinuation. "That's none of your business."

He tossed the papers on my desk. "This is."

I considered throwing them back at him, but I'd had phone calls from board members who either begged or admonished me to get along with William for the benefit of the company. I knew he was involved with another woman. His morning coffee visits had ceased in the last few weeks. When we had to discuss a project, we would soon find ourselves in a heated argument. It did not go unnoticed. Employees had asked me if they were still going to have jobs.

William was currently working on a coronary artery clip, a device to assist surgeons when they remove a damaged section of vessel to perform anastomosis, the sewing of two vessels back together. Briefly it floated into my mind how ironic it was that we worked on devices to heal the heart, yet we couldn't heal matters of our own hearts.

"What do you need from me?" I picked up the papers. "I thought you completed this?"

"I'm working out a few flaws. I'll have it ready for the board meeting." He said it as though this would make or break the outcome of the meeting. I'd had enough. I couldn't help myself. "Do you think you'll be awarded a gold star, William?" I threw the papers at him. "Do you really think you can run this company? You can't find your glasses half the time. It takes incredible effort on my part just to keep you focused long enough to complete a project. I tried to persuade other companies to hire you, but your drunken belligerence precedes you. Your precious reputation has been tarnished."

"You're a bitch. Your days are numbered here."

"Get out."

Paula opened the door and announced, "This meeting is over." She stood guard, waiting for William to exit. He threw a look of disgust at us, left the documents on the floor, and stalked out. Paula was a tiger when it came to her mother.

"Are you OK?"

"Yes."

"Do you think you should lie down? Do you want to go home? We can handle things here."

"I think I will leave now."

I was exhausted. If I had known how to find the place in the foothills where Lynn had taken me for lunch when I was in the rehabilitation center, I would have gone there. Instead I headed home. Parker ran up the drive to greet me. Her unconditional love soothed me. I sat on the porch and threw a few balls for her. At least I could make her happy. The phone rang but I didn't have the energy to answer. The Rocky Mountain plains sunset began its spectacular light show. Parker and I stayed on the porch to watch the sky change from lemon yellow to flamingo pink, then bursting into fiery reds. The distant horizon became smudged with charcoal silhouettes of mountain peaks.

I went in and found the message machine blinking. I sighed and decided to use the bathroom before I listened to the numerous messages.

I perched on a stool, pushed play, and Lynn's voice erupted in the room. "I didn't mean what I said. I'm sorry." Click. "Will you call me at the office when you get home? It's Wednesday. Can I come out?" Click. "Do you hate me? Are you ever going to talk to me again? I feel betrayed. You have a whole other life." Click. "Please call. I'm so sorry. I miss you."

I stopped the machine. She was trying to pull me in again. I just felt tired. I really didn't want to listen anymore, but I pushed play. It was Samantha. "Hello, gorgeous. I tried your office and your daughter, I assume, told me you'd gone home. When I think of last evening, a frisson of excitement runs through my body. I'd like to see you again. Let's plan a trip. How about camping? Think about it and I'll catch you later." Click.

I smiled.

The phone rang. Hesitantly I picked it up. "Hello?"

"I've tried and tried to reach you," Lynn said.

"Yes, I know."

"Do you want to talk to me?"

"Lynn, you called it quits and left."

"I didn't mean it. I was angry. I thought you and she . . ."

"Spent the night together?"

"Yes."

"We did." Moments of silence. "How do you think I've felt knowing that you and Dick still sleep together?"

"Diana, it's different. We're married."

"Different? Am I your mistress?" I choked on a laugh, then went on sadly, "The feelings you had last night I've had for a long time. It hurts. I don't want my life to be so complicated, either."

"But . . ."

"You've had both of us wrapped around your little finger." I realized I was angry, very angry. "No more of this for me, Lynn; it's time to decide. Are you leaving Dick?"

"Diana, I love you."

"That wasn't my question."

"I'm working it out."

"We bought this place so we could be together. Is that real for you?"

"I want it to be."

"So you can honestly say that you plan to leave Dick?"

"You said you wouldn't pressure me."

I couldn't believe it. And still I listened for another 20 minutes. Her evasions and excuses multiplied. The more she squirmed, the greater grew my anger and disgust. She was pitiful. I finally reached my limit.

"Lynn, when I get the divorce settlement from William, I should be able to buy you out."

She began to whine. "I don't want to be bought out. It's our place."

"It's not our place until you live here."

"I want to be with you."

"I will not be a hostage to your selfish games." My words rushed out as though a dam had burst. "I'm not a pawn on your chess board anymore. We'll have to try to be friends and business associates. I don't know what else to do." I was in tears now and so was she. "I'll pack your things, or you and Dick can have the place to yourselves this weekend to gather your stuff." I let a teensy barb fly. "He should enjoy that."

I didn't know how to end the conversation and apparently she didn't, either. We were silent for some time. I broke the impasse. "You can let me know tomorrow. I'm really tired. I need to go now. Please don't call me anymore today." She hung up.

I sat for a long time, allowing myself to fully accept the stand I had just taken. Everything I had told her I should have said long before. I'm sure Ms. Tiener would agree. I decided to see her again soon.

The phone rang again. I picked it up, ready to tell Lynn I would turn it off if she continued to call. Luckily Samantha's voice came through before I began to rant. "There's a whole group of women going camping the second weekend in June. I think you'd really enjoy it. Would you like to go?"

"Sounds like fun. I'd love to."

"Diana, are you all right?"

"Yes. Well, actually I'm exhausted."

"Is there anything I can do?"

"You already have and thank you."

"Call if you need anything, OK?"

"Sure. Let's talk soon."

"You bet. I've got you on my mind."

I laughed. "I can see why Ann has a hard time keeping up with you."

I could hear the smile in Samantha's voice. "You're as much of a dynamo as I am."

After we said our goodbyes, I realized it had been a very long time since I had felt so unabashedly desired. Despite my weariness I felt energized. And a little sassy.

# CHAPTER TWENTY-FIVE

I STARED OUT the window in Ms. Tiener's waiting room.

"Diana?"

Ms. Tiener stood beside my chair. I hadn't heard her approach. I rose and followed her into the office.

"You seemed very far away in the waiting room," she said after the courteous check-in talk. "Where did you go?"

I pondered how to tell her about the showdown with Lynn. She waited.

"Lynn is moving out of our ranch this weekend."

"She came to this decision? Or did you?"

"I pushed her because I needed to know if she really intended ever to leave Dick. It was horrible. She wouldn't say it. She chose her husband."

"How do you feel about that?"

"Both hurt and relieved. I don't want Lynn or anyone else to make me feel I'm not worth the effort to build a loving, respectful, devoted relationship. I'm done with selling myself short."

"Write down ten attributes you would use to describe your ideal life partner."

I began scribbling in my dragonfly journal. This was fun. My pen flew over the paper with words like committed, devoted, intelligent, ambitious, compassionate, self-assured, affectionate, romantic, passionate, open-minded, dignified, clean, respectful, and a non-smoker.

"A woman?"

"Definitely."

I added lesbian to my list.

"Now, Diana, mark the ones you believe are absolute. The 80 percent that is non-negotiable."

I did, then laughed. "I'm pretty demanding. I circled almost everything on the list."

"You have a right to be. It's your life. This is your personal guide book. It will help you choose a more suitable mate."

I remembered another item to add to my list: she must smell like luscious fruit.

"You're smiling."

"It's a grand list."

IT WAS THE night before the board meeting. Sleep eluded me. I paced, mentally ticking off the goals Pioneering had accomplished over the past year despite my illness. William still harbored the idea that he could usurp me and assume command. Our business tug of war over power was a replica of our marriage.

The next morning a virulent blend of aftershave, perfume, and anxious sweat permeated the conference room. The scent of blood added a primitive base note as the members of the board circled around the elegant walnut conference table. The timeless game of predator and prey had begun. Paula cranked up the air conditioner before she left the room. I took my place at the long table that had once been a symbol of success. Now it was the feeding ground. I called the meeting to order. My plan had been to extol our accomplishments, but I was headed off at the pass.

Bob stood. My eyes narrowed. My nose twitched. The battle had begun. I could feel perspiration trickle down my spine. Why had the board chosen Bob to deliver their mandate? His only qualification for being present was that he was married to Marcia, a voting member of the board. We used him as an advisor on government regulations when we had to determine new product feasibility.

I had formed the board of directors with three women—Lynn, Marcia, and I—and two men—William and Harris, a highly respected cardiovascular surgeon. The term glass ceiling had not yet been popularized, but was beginning to be spoken by feminist writers. At that time a woman climbing the corporate ladder could get as far as mid-level management before her head hit the invisible barrier of gender discrimination. I had already gone beyond my expected role when I became a mechanical engineer and designed a heart valve. I continued my ascent beyond the crystal vault, a phrase George Sand, French author and feminist, coined in 1839: "I was a woman; for suddenly my wings collapsed, closed in around my head like an impenetrable crystal vault and I fell . . . " when I formed my own medical device engineering and manufacturing company. Unfortunately, I had learned that being a woman did not mean an inherent alliance with other women. Marcia was as malicious and ruthless as any man when it came to power. Bob was her manservant.

I halted my speech. "Yes?"

Bob cleared his throat. "The board has voted to replace you"—He paused to glance at William, then returned his nervous gaze back to me—"and William."

I don't know what my face showed, but I will never forget William's look of absolute shock. His ego had been trampled. The undermining and deceitful innuendos and accusations he had perpetuated to dismantle my power had backfired. He was taken out by his own venom. I watched while all this played over his features as accusations of our mismanagement were listed, as though we were criminals being indicted. Bob's voice droned on. "We've had numerous complaints about you and William. It is in the best interests of this company and the shareholders for you both to resign."

Whom should I annihilate first? William the peevish worm? Marcia the barracuda? Lynn the coward? Harris, another entitled male? Had I landed in Oz? William was the pseudo wizard whose illusions duped most, including himself. I was Dorothy, the small-town girl who fearlessly exposed the lies, and with tenacious determination established rightful leadership. I wanted to scream. Who do these people think they are? Without me there is no Pioneering.

I needed air. William had gone from ghostly pale to cherry red. I thought, he's going to have a coronary. What perfect karmic justice, given his belief that his coronary artery clip project would secure his seat at the helm.

I curbed my vengeful thoughts and grabbed the sleeve of his suit. "Let's go."

He gave me an incredulous look.

I tugged again. "Let's go for a walk."

"Now?" he managed to squeak.

"Right now," I said.

William stood. I led him toward the door, shooting words like bullets as we left the conference room. "There is no company without us. You can't replace us. You don't have the votes." I shot a look at Lynn, who was flushed. I couldn't tell if it was shame or anger. I glared in Marcia's direction. "Your attempt to overthrow me is contemptible." Then my corporate ladylike manners made me say, "Please enjoy the refreshments."

William and I passed Paula at her desk. Her mouth had fallen open and she stared at me. William kept moving while he mopped his face with his handkerchief. He opened the door for me.

"Honey, please just go and make sure no one leaves," I told Paula. "We'll be back shortly."

I followed William. He took off his suit coat and rolled up his sleeves. He tossed his tie over his shoulder and offered me his arm. Still gallant. I needed the support. My legs were quaking. We walked the path that circled the pond.

"I didn't see that coming," William said.

"I'll bet," I retorted.

I told him that I had known about his takeover attempt. True to form he didn't apologize or even attempt to look ashamed.

"I was afraid you were going to lose the company. You were acting crazy. Not at all like yourself." He glanced sideways at me. "Still aren't."

"All you accomplished was to cause a panic," I said. "They're trying to force our hand."

"What are we going to do?"

"They know they can't remove us," I said. "It's a ploy. I want some time to consider our options. Do you think we can stay civil long enough to hammer out a plan in 30 days?"

He pretended to consider my proposal. I'm certain that, if he hadn't just had the bombastic shit kicked out of him he would have disagreed. I watched him inwardly surrender.

"I think that will work."

We finished our circuit around the peace pond. I stuck my hand out to him. He took it. Together we returned to the conference room and delivered our decision. Meanwhile, I had 30 days to devise an exit plan.


LYNN CONTINUED TO hound me with incessant phone calls. She staked a financial claim to the ranch, maintaining that she did not want our deal to end. Why did I think she had invested in land out in the middle of nowhere? I wanted to pay her off, but William still hadn't sold the house. Her things were gone but she still had a key. She stowed an emergency overnight case there for her visits to her investment. Conversations became interrogations about who I was seeing and bringing to the ranch. She voiced her righteous condemnation of the strangers that I let invade our private sanctuary. I, on the other hand, was enjoying my freedom and new lifestyle.

One day at the office Lynn asked if I would join her after work for a cappuccino, her treat. In a nanosecond I thought, what's the harm in a coffee? I wanted to steer our relationship back to a professional alliance and team camaraderie.

Our coffee meet was a disaster, at least for me. I noticed that nothing had changed except that I clearly saw that Lynn could not think for herself. Her husband did the thinking and she acquiesced. I also observed how Lynn manipulated to get what she wanted. She whined and pouted.

After the coffee meet I took out my dragonfly journal. I wrote a list of Lynn's attributes and compared them to my relationship guidelines. I put my analytical engineering mind to work. I used the 80/20 relationship ratio that Ms. Tiener had suggested to calculate our percentages. It came out to 60/40. I shook my head. I kicked myself for the role I played in our affair. The desire I used to have for Lynn had become heartache. It was not good for either of us.

My next task was to work out a plan to split the company with William. We began to discuss the options. The new woman in his life attended our business meetings. She had a slew of lawyers she offered to us to help achieve an equitable outcome. Her interest was, of course, to protect William.

The revenues from product sales had not increased quickly enough to meet the increased expenses of the new facility. I began to seek out manufacturing contracts on devices that we didn't design or develop. We had a government-approved facility with regulations and procedural specifications already in place. This separate division would provide another revenue stream.

An idea began to form. I would take over the custom manufacturing division. William would take the patents and the products we already sold, along with the customer base. He could deal with the board and the shareholders.

It was probably the worst business deal I had ever made. However, it allowed me to start over. I was a divorced lesbian, free to do as I pleased. Life had just become a helluva lot less complicated. I was ready for my next adventure. To camp with a pack of wild women.

# CHAPTER TWENTY-SIX

MY OFFICE HAD REI bags scattered on the floor. I had to replace all the gear that I lost on the camping trip with Lynn.

Paula came in and eyed the results of my shopping expedition. "Mom?" I knew at least four questions were implied. Where are you going? Who are you going with? Are you strong enough? It's not Lynn, is it? I told her my plan to go camping with Samantha's group.

She visibly relaxed. "I'm so glad to see you happy."

"I'm fortunate to have you for my daughter."

"How could I stop loving you? You're my mother. If my child was gay, I wouldn't stop loving him. Isn't love just love?"

I smiled at her with pride. Her wholehearted love for animals and their devotion to her must be the source of such wisdom. "You should start a support group for adult children of gays and lesbians."

She looked at me, horrified and then we both laughed.

"I wish I could see your brother."

"Give it time," she said. "He's caught up in himself right now. He loves you; he'll come around."

I knew that meant that she would use her influence on him.


CAMPING WITH A group of wild women was fun, but it was different in more ways than I had anticipated. It was not exactly my idea of wilderness camping. We took short day hikes, spent time reading, went fishing in a nearby pond or sat around telling tales. It was more like a lesbian camping fiesta with frequent siestas. Some were noisily amorous.

When I hiked I was careful to monitor my endurance. I did well downhill and on flat terrain, but uphill strained my body.

My legs had become stronger. I wanted to push hard and test my limits, but the fear of having spasms made me behave.

When the sun began its descent, everyone gathered to cook dinner and party. If someone had caught fish it was fried and shots of tequila circled. A couple of women brought guitars, which they played while fires were kept stoked high, both the actual fires and the sexual ones. Samantha did not hide her attraction for me. It made me uncomfortable to show affection to her in front of Ann. I noticed that Ann would disappear early from the fireside. I could imagine how seeing her partner with someone else would hurt. I valued my friendships and social relationships with all the women more than I wanted to sleep with Samantha.

When I got home I realized a seed had been planted. The mountains and I had a date. I wanted to complete my wilderness quest. This time it was going to be solo. I started to do more vigorous body workouts to prepare. I practiced climbing by adding more treks up and down the stairs in the house. My daily chores at the farm helped.

Lynn accosted me one day at the office. We were still in the process of dismantling the company. She had heard about my upcoming trip and tried to wheedle her way into coming along. Her first tactic was to attack my health. I fended her off. Then she tried to seduce me. If we spent time alone back out in the wilderness, it could rekindle our passion. She even hinted that it would sever her link to Dick. I told her it was my personal quest, I needed to overcome the lingering defeat I felt. To revisit physically, mentally, or emotionally the journey I had taken with her would not change the outcome. I would take only Parker. Lynn argued that I was too bullheaded for my own good. I told her she should look in the mirror.

Although I had resisted her pleading, twinges of regret plagued me. How easily she reignited my yearning for that dream. I redirected my temptation into scheduling a visit with Ms. Tiener.

The day before I was leaving for my solo wilderness quest, I saw Ms. Tiener. I recounted the camping fiesta and how I felt being with Samantha while Ann was there.

"Was it the same feeling you experienced around Lynn and Dick?" she asked after I was done.

"I will not be used as a Band-Aid for marital boredom," I said heatedly.

"Not on your list of compromises?"

I shook my head. "When I wrote about it in my journal, I was led to another aha! moment. Both my husbands had cheated on me. In essence so had Lynn. I knew what this kind of betrayal felt like. How could I do that to someone else?"

"I'm glad you saw the connection."

We took a break to pour and sip tea. "I'm very curious about something."

"Tell me," she said.

"How did you come up with your relationship ratio?"

She smiled. "It came out of a relationship-building class that I took early in my career. An assignment was to make our wish list for the ideal partner, and include defining what was absolutely non-negotiable and what was acceptable. I used the same technique with my clients, as I did with you, and a pattern emerged. I have an analytical mind so I applied a percentage to the proportion of absolutes, what I call our basic nature, and the attributes that we can compromise on. I noticed that when the ratio landed in the range of 70/30 or 80/20, relationships were stronger. There wasn't an undercurrent of resentment. Remember, even if your list shows a 70/30 ratio, it's only 15 percent that each partner has to be willing to concede. When the ratios got down to 60/40, devotion became toleration."

I was taking notes, trying to capture what she said for later reflection. I looked up when I realized she had stopped.

"There is so much suffering in the world that we don't have control over, but we can control our impulses and how we relate to each other. Why cause pain, to ourselves or to someone else?

"It sounds like common sense, the way you describe it," I said. "Why don't we all know this?"

"Each of us comes into the world and grows up with our own unique set of circumstances. Our upbringing, the environment, cultural beliefs, even imprints from the past contribute to our development. So much shapes our responses to life. I just strive to be as accountable in my life as I teach others to be. How else could I be an effective counselor?"

"It's the Golden Rule: treat others the way you want to be treated." I murmured. "Maybe I should take that class."

Ms. Tiener held out a card. "I thought you might say that."

It read, *Relationship Building 101, Dr. Bernie DeCoke.*

When I said goodbye to Ms. Tiener it felt as though we had finished our therapist client relationship. I hoped that we would have opportunities to see each other socially. I wanted to meet her partner someday. She was the kind of friend I would be honored to have in my life. I didn't say this to her. I decided to let the future unfold naturally.

I went home to pack. It was going to be a three-day and two-night trip. I had bought the lightest possible pack. I was taking granola bars, dehydrated food for warm meals, a one-person single-season tube tent, an aluminum pot to boil water, a knife, and plastic utensils. Parker roamed through my little piles strewn on the floor. I was checking each item before I stowed it in the backpack. I was scared. I hoped I could manage. I'd worked hard at convincing myself and others that I was capable.

The phone rang. I answered, thinking it would be Paula. It was Lynn. I considered hanging up as she began to plead, but how could I do that after my session with Ms. Tiener. I could hear Lynn's desperation.

"Lynn, if I thought my health was a problem, I wouldn't go. I would not put myself in danger. I know the repercussions." I paused

She charged in with, "I'll follow a quarter-mile behind you. I won't bother you. But just in case, I'll be there."

I remembered Paula's comments about Lynn's creepy lurking. On one hand it gave her the ability to be a kick-ass quality assurance manager. On the other she used her spidey sense to manipulate and control. Was this what Ms. Tiener meant when she said we can control our impulses? We can choose to use our skills to benefit the good of all, or extort others for our own selfish gains.

"No!" I said in a raised voice. "This topic is not up for further discussion. "You've chosen Dick as your life partner, not me. Whether I understand, agree, or like it doesn't matter. We are now coworkers and, if we can handle it, friends."

"Please, just meet me for breakfast before you leave. I have something to give you."

I reluctantly agreed to meet her at the gas station near the ranch at 8 a.m. I needed to get gas anyway. I hung up.

Parker lay her head in my lap. I stroked her. It settled me a bit. I wasn't desperate anymore. I wasn't hopeless anymore. I didn't have to give more than I wanted to give of myself. I finished the packing. I lay snuggled in my soft, cozy bedding, wondering why I was willingly going to lie on the hard ground and freeze. I was scared shitless to be alone on the mountain in the pitch dark. And Parker was no better than I was at reading a map.

The next morning I was up at dawn. One more thorough check of my backpack, and I then loaded Parker. We headed to the gas station. Lynn was already there when I pulled up to the pump. I got out and started to fill the tank. She met me, her eyes red, shoulders sagging, holding a gift wrapped package. She tried to hug me. I busied myself with the gas nozzle.

"I had no idea how much I love you," she cried, "how much I need to be close to you."

"Lynn, go home to Dick. I don't need an escort, a bodyguard, a when-her-husband-allows-it lover." Her face was pale and she appeared beaten. I curbed my urge to shock her with a cattle prod. It was a good thing it wasn't on board.

She handed her gift to me. "Please read it while you're out there. I hope it will help you understand."

I replaced the nozzle and took the package. "Thank you."

"Call me the minute you get home. You know I won't rest until you do."

She shuffled back to the jeep. I got in the car just in time. I unwrapped the package. It was a book, *The Bridges of Madison County*. I didn't recognize it. I tucked it in the backpack and got on the road.

I arrived in the parking lot at the campground. Three other vehicles were already there even though it was still early in the morning. The trailhead had the parched high summer color rather than the rich jewel tones of fall. Other than that it was much the same. How could it have changed so little, while my life was so radically altered?

Parker stood still to let me put on her doggy pack. With our gear in place we walked the wide path to the creek. I remembered how young Parker had been. Now she scurried across the creek, all grown up with none of her puppy antics.

The sky was a cloudless azure. I took a deep breath. No dizziness. No fuzzy head. No leaden exhaustion. Just pure clean mountain air with traces of camp smoke, propane gas, and lots of pine trees.

Three miles from where I wanted to camp I sat for a break. The water in my canteen was cool. The granola bar tasted bland but it was filling. I took out the book and began to read. To me it was the story of a discontented housewife. I guess that must have been Lynn. It was depressing. Back in my pack it went. One more drink and Parker and I were back on the trail. There were two tents already pitched where Lynn and I had stayed the first night. We walked on. This part of the trail seemed unfamiliar. After another third of a mile we found an unoccupied area big enough for my small tent. It was protected by some rocks and had a small fire pit.

I staked the four corners of the tube tent, using a small rock for a hammer. After tying the cord from the front peak to a tree, I felt the assembly was complete. With the sleeping bag unrolled there were only a few inches of clearance all the way around.

Firewood was plentiful and easy to gather. I stacked it and set up a kindling tipi in the fire pit for later use. I had done well. The exhaustion I felt was not unusual, considering the distance we had come.

Grinning, I patted Parker. "We're doing it, girl."

She wagged her butt as I stroked her. Then she flopped on her back for a belly rub.

Dusk crept in. I grabbed my pack to dig out the matches. I was looking forward to my rehydrated freeze-dried dinner pouch. I always packed matches in different places in case one got wet or wouldn't work. I searched the side pouch. Nothing. I unzipped the back. My probing netted the same result. This wasn't possible.

"Diana," I said to myself. "You screwed up big time. Maybe you weren't ready for this trip. Don't panic. It's getting dark. It's too late to find other campers. Shit." I can't spend the night alone in the mountains without a fire. No fire to keep animals away. No way to boil water for a hot meal or refill my canteen. Parker had dog chow from her pack. I looked at the hard little rounds of chow, but dismissed that crunchy idea. I also decided against the dry version of the dinner pouch. I would have to settle for a granola bar and water for supper. My stomach moaned. I could picture the matches on the floor when I was packing. Did Parker carry them off?

I pawed through everything and finally found them in a zip-loc bag rolled up in my pajamas. What had I been thinking? My panic subsided. Parker watched my every move. She was a wonderful companion. She believed in me. She didn't panic.

I lit the campfire. Suddenly a wave of gratitude washed over me for the simplicity. The boiling water, the meal in a pouch, the crackle and warmth of the fire were wonderful. The stars were as plentiful as they always are. The muted sounds from other campers made me feel safe, not invaded. Parker was beside me. Her demands were also simple. Did the previous disastrous trek occur to topple me from my high and mighty perch? Did it really have to be such a steep fall?

The chill of the mountain air seeped in, and I decided it was time to crawl into bed. I banked the fire and tidied up. I crammed my pack into the tent, pushed Parker in and crawled after her. I shivered and pulled my now potty-trained partner closer in the sleeping bag. We were in this together. I tried to read another chapter, but holding the book with a penlight stuck between my lips became too much effort.

As I lay there with Parker's warm body pulled tight to me, I could hear critters scurrying about and chewing nearby twigs. Some were little faint sounds. Other sounds were louder as animal bodies actually brushed the sides of the tent as they passed. Parker became restless with every noise. She wanted to check each one out. Mostly I restrained her. Sometimes I couldn't. She would wiggle out of the bag and bark at the noise. After reassuring Parker and myself that the noises were nothing to be alarmed about, I slept some. The long night lingered on and on. Every time I woke I'd look for the light of morning so I'd know we'd survived the night.

The next day I would face the boulder field. I began to perspire and tremble at the thought of it. Parker squirmed. I held her tight. I reassured myself that I was much healthier than I was the last time. I'd only be carrying a day pack. I could leave the rest here at my base camp. Still it seemed formidable.

I awoke to the rustling of branches and a scraping against the tent. Parker was growling, low and deep. I held my breath until the need for air made me quietly inhale and slowly exhale. I listened carefully, sorting out Parker's throaty rumbles, my restricted breathing, and the sounds in the darkness. By the time it seemed as if the beast had gone, I was shivering. I put on all the clothing I could find and got re-situated in the sleeping bag.

It sounded like a deer. Right. It wasn't a bear. Parker and I lay quietly until darkness began to lift. It was too cold to shed our protective cocoon, so we drifted in and out of sleep until another noise brought us fully awake. The sun was up.

"Are you ready for some hot breakfast?" I asked Parker.

We had survived our first night. It was 8:30 before I made our camp shipshape. I reorganized the day pack with water, binoculars, the dragonfly journal, leftover stew, a couple of dog biscuits, and the book. I carefully placed the matches in their plastic bag in the zippered side pouch. Parker and I trekked on. In just minutes I was facing the boulder field. I could see horses skirting along its edge a mile or so away.

The first steps onto those monster rocks were the hardest. The memory of the physical agony I had suffered caused more trembling in my legs than the strain of the climb. I moved with determination up and over the boulders. Parker zigzagged easily through. When I finally stood on flat ground and looked back at the expanse of giant rocks, I was pleased at the ease with which I had crossed. It hadn't been that big a deal.

The path was worn and jagged as it followed the creek. When meeting or being passed by the occasional hiker, we'd engage in a short conversation. The upper portion of the trail was less traveled and more difficult because of its steepness, endless switchbacks, and fallen trees that cluttered the path. You had to snake around and through the limbs. My legs were shaking but I sensed I was near the crest. I trudged on.

Finally I was overlooking the box canyon, the place where I had been trapped before. An overwhelming sense of relief surged through me. Pent up tears flowed freely. I stood, thanking God for the strength to achieve this victory.

Here I was, against all odds. I was drinking in the wonder of this planet. The sun was so vibrant it washed out the rich blue of the sky, the mountainous horizon that stretched out as far as I could see, the wildflower-bedecked meadows below, the fully leafed aspen trees and the grasses thick and tall, waving on the warm breeze.

It was summer in its full glory. After experiencing near death I was now very much alive. I was here. I had made it. My quest was accomplished.

I sat on a rock that gave me a full view of the canyon. I panned the area with my binoculars, tracing my journey with Lynn. The magnificent beaver pond was missing. Had it been a hallucination? I thought not. I hadn't seen it while hiking the trail. There was a new marker at the base of the narrow trail that traversed the ridge. I believed several yards beyond that had been our turnaround point. Perhaps the beaver dam had been removed and the sign replaced. What an amazing perspective I now had. From this height the scary boulders looked more like friendly stones. I sat back against the sun-warmed rock when I had my fill of the vista. Now I would eat and regroup.

I ate the morning leftovers and gave Parker a couple of dog biscuits. I made myself comfortable so I could finish Lynn's book. The story had changed from depressing to happy; but like so many things, it was how it ended that mattered. I read on.

By early afternoon I had finished. It was the story of a chance meeting that erupted into a passionate love affair between a famous photographer and an Iowa farm wife. I knew that heat and that longing. The pain of their parting was close to my own pain. How could she not leave her husband? Her monotonous life? How could they bury their love and yet yearn for each other until his death 14 years later? What a waste, and what a pathetic ending. I felt angry. Lynn picked this book for me to read on my journey to heal. Her choice seemed manipulative. Was she being intentionally hurtful? Her commitment to an empty marriage was a decision I couldn't admire.

I finally let go of so many aspects of my life. Like climbing the giant boulder field, I had climbed up and over many obstacles. The journey served to intensify my passion for opportunities that lay ahead. There was no way I was going to waste my life. I had a class to sign up for when I returned home.

### The End and The Beginning

## Disclaimer

Some names and other identifying aspects have been changed to respect the privacy of some of the characters mentioned within these pages. This memoir represents the authors best efforts to accurately remember the events of nearly 30 years ago, despite numerous illness-related hallucinations and medically-induced drug-altered states of awareness.

Diana Wright is a visionary who views her life as a blank canvas meant to be rendered in audacious color. She was born in 1947 and grew up on a farm in rural Minnesota. Balancing full time work, part time school, parenting, and being a wife to a Vietnam veteran, after nine years she earned her degree in biological science at CSU Fullerton. She went on to engineer medical devices and later founded her own medical device manufacturing company. Diana worked with a heart surgeon in London, oversaw production facilities in Holland and coordinated with a world wide salesforce. She bravely shares a segment of her story here so that others might create their own portrait of vitality.

Dr. Bernie DeCoke grew up in Colorado, where she obtained an MA in Psychology/Guidance & Counseling from the University of Northern Colorado. She became a college instructor and therapist, a warrior with a mission to help students and clients build a core of dignity and self-respect. Later, she merged the body, mind and spirit triad she believes necessary for total health with doctorates in Naturopathy and Metaphysics. Bernie perfectly complements Diana's voice and contributes much to interpreting Diana's story.

Together Diana and Bernie form a bond that reflects the hero attributes of keen intelligence, shrewd determination, astute courage, outstanding accomplishments and generous compassion. We can never read too many stories with the power to ignite our own inherent warrior, visionary, or hero. Currently the two live on a small ranch in Colorado, where they tackle a myriad of creative projects, including the building of a full-size covered wagon–just for fun.

Their website is: http://www.wrightwithdecoke.com